Leg Up
The Courage to Dream

*"Leg Up Farm is a masterpiece:
a place of therapy, healing, and spirit."*

Nancy Englehart

*"Leg Up Farm is a life-changing gift
of love and care for so many families."*

Mike Ovadia, Parent

"Leg Up Farm is like family."

Alexander, Twelve-Year-Old

*"It is amazing to work at a place
where miracles happen every day."*

Tim Keiner, Leg Up Farm Staff Member

*"What an amazing place this is for everyone...
Leg Up Farm gave me my child back."*

Marianne Luca, Parent

"Leg Up Farm gives children the confidence they need to be able to push forward and know that they're doing their best, and that it's good enough."

Laurie Hazel, Parent

"Leg Up Farm is a very special therapy facility. It's a place where families are fully embraced and children are given the chance to discover their abilities. There are no limitations at Leg Up Farm."

Susan Hubley, Highmark

"What I liked was that, right from our first meeting, the staff addressed questions to my granddaughter, asking her what she felt about therapy. They respected what she had to say as well as what I had to say."

Saleem Muhaimin, Grandparent

"Because of Louie's dream, our son has a hopeful future. He has come such a long way at Leg Up Farm. It takes people like the staff there to help our little man walk straighter and live more confidently."

Kathleen and David Breault, Parents

"Leg Up Farm changed our family members' lives."

Diana Spangler, Parent

"Having everything under one roof makes it so much simpler for the parent. It takes the stress off having to travel from one place to another. It's also comforting to come to a place where it's not all business, since Leg Up Farm treats everybody like a family member. They truly care about your child. They watch them grow. And it's as important to them as it is to you."

Amy Campisi, Parent

"I've been a Leg Up Farm volunteer almost since its inception. To see the project go from a great idea, to plans on paper, to a building fulfilling dreams is truly overwhelming."

Jennifer Frey, Leg Up Farm Volunteer

"I definitely see a difference in the parents from the moment they walk through the door."

Melissa Maley, Leg Up Farm Staff Member

Leg Up
The Courage to Dream

Louis J. Castriota, Jr.

Blooming Twig Books
New York / Tulsa

LEG UP: The Courage to Dream
Copyright © 2013 Louis J. Castriota, Jr.
www.louiecastriota.com

Back cover photograph courtesy of:
The Susquehanna Photographic

Published by:
Blooming Twig Books
New York / Tulsa
www.bloomingtwig.com

All rights reserved. This book may not be photocopied for personal or professional use. No part of this book may be reproduced, stored in a retrieval system, or transmitted in any form or by any means (electronic, mechanical, photocopying, recording, or otherwise) without permission in writing from the author and/or publisher.

Hardcover: ISBN 978-1-61343-023-1

Paperback: ISBN 978-1-61343-171-9

eBook: ISBN 978-1-61343-024-8

Dedicated

*to Laurie, Olivia, Toby,
Brooke and Lauren —
you are my special gifts,*

*and to Mom and Dad for
teaching me to be compassionate
and caring toward others.*

Table of Contents

Foreword 15

Louie's Note to the Reader 19

Preface 23

Chapter 1   Cookin' Up Love 31
              Our summer romance

Chapter 2   Giddy Up, Gal 39
              Mom was right all along

Chapter 3   Too Close to Home? 45
              A surprising arrangement

Chapter 4   Small Miracles 53
              Welcome, Brooke

Chapter 5   I Will Survive 59
              Coming to terms with a different future

Chapter 6   Can We Go Yet? 67
              Trying to be everywhere at once

Chapter 7   Question Everything 71
              The idea that wouldn't go away

Chapter 8   The Courage to Dream 79
              Following your heart no matter what

Chapter 9	Visualize Your End Goal as Reality 83	
	Keeping the dream alive	
Insert	Live the Dream S1	
	A special section dedicated to all of the children that inspire me every day.	
Chapter 10	Focus on the Next Step 91	
	Finding my own path	
Chapter 11	Ch-Ch-Ch Changes 97	
	Doing what it takes	
Chapter 12	Do the Right Things Every Day 103	
	My favorite DJ	
Chapter 13	A Bureaucratic Angel 111	
	Friends in high places	
Chapter 14	Land Free for the Asking 117	
	A long time coming	
Chapter 15	Step by Step 123	
	A view from the front porch	
Chapter 16	A Spirit of Giving 127	
	Honoring Matthew	
Chapter 17	Work at the Dream 131	
	Pony rides, clowns, & lottery tickets	
Chapter 18	Never Stop Believing 137	
	In it for the long haul	
Chapter 19	The Last Puzzle Pieces 143	
	Breaking new ground	

Chapter 20 A New Vision 151
  The dream becomes real

Afterword 157

Acknowledgments 167

About Leg Up Farm 171

Foreword

In early 1998, just after I had left Pennsylvania state government, I was approached by my friend Marie, who asked whether I might be able to give someone named Louie Castriota some advice. She told me that Louie was looking for state funds and needed some assistance searching for contacts. I agreed to meet him at Marie's home, not far away from my own.

We sat in Marie's kitchen, and Louie gave me a heartfelt presentation. He brought artist renderings, and he explained his vision and various challenges in great detail. Although Louie was very persuasive, and the idea behind Leg Up Farm was great, I admit that I had very little confidence that it would ever come to fruition. His would be a herculean task, and he explained that he was working full-time, raising a young family, and facing other daunting hurdles. Clearly, I wrote him off too early. At that point, I really did not know the depth of his commitment and ability to carry out his vision.

I lost track of Louie for about ten years, although I would hear occasional rumblings about Leg Up Farm. Each time, I would think to myself, "How charming," or "He certainly is tenacious with this dream." Still, I didn't believe Louie's dream would ever be realized.

Many years later, while I was sitting on the board of a local community bank, we began discussing opportunities that would be arising at Leg Up Farm, which had recently opened its doors to the public. I recalled my earlier conversation with Louie, and I needed to see whether he had truly brought his dream to fruition. I got in my car and decided to see this place for myself.

After meandering through gorgeous countryside, I was stunned when I drove up to an amazing facility in a wonderful setting. Louie welcomed me, and, although I was a drop-in guest, he gave me a thorough tour. He excitedly showed me their therapy rooms, their integrated play and classroom space, their riding arenas and all of the animals. Most important, throughout the facility, I saw families and their children all feeling at home and valued. Without advertising, Leg Up Farm already worked with over 400 families, who now knew that they were not alone and that their future was bright.

The following quote by American anthropologist Margaret Mead applies directly to Louie Castriota and Leg Up Farm and what they have accomplished for families and children in our community: "Never doubt that a small group of thoughtful, committed citizens can change the world. Indeed, it is the only thing that ever has."

Louie inspires everyone around him and motivates them to achieve a shared vision of improving care for children with special needs. While many of us dream of winning the lottery or taking a grand trip, Louie and everyone at Leg Up Farm invest their time and spirit on behalf of others. They see problems and solutions where others accept mediocrity and fragmented care.

Louie has a profound devotion to his own family and to his new family at Leg Up Farm. His focus is the promise of securing a better future for his children and for children all around the country. Since the day I "rediscovered" Louie Castriota and Leg Up Farm, I have learned about commitment and vision, if even just by osmosis! Louie cares deeply for others, and thinks about every little detail while never losing sight of the big picture. He is not afraid to re-imagine the future and create the pathway to achieve his goals. I have seen a window into Louie's expanded vision, and this is just the beginning.

The stories on these pages are inspiring, just as Leg Up Farm is inspiring. But this book is also something more: it is a blueprint for each of us to create a vision in our own lives, and then work hard to make that vision a reality.

Wanda D. Filer, M.D., M.B.A.

Dr. Wanda Filer is a family physician and founder of the Strategic Health Institute, which builds awareness of today's health issues and the need for change. She served as the first Physician General of Pennsylvania. Dr. Filer was also a health correspondent for WGAL-TV, the NBC affiliate in Lancaster, for 18 years. She is active nationally and locally, lecturing extensively and advocating for underserved populations.

Dr. Filer has won many awards for her health advocacy efforts, especially around immunization, cancer control and the prevention of family violence.

Leg Up Farm Ribbon Cutting, 2010.

Louie's Note to the Reader

This dream started as the attempt by one dad to help his little girl. That little girl is my daughter Brooke, who happens to have special healthcare needs.

Since we opened the doors to Leg Up Farm, not only have I seen a change in Brooke, I have been blessed by seeing the Farm change the lives of thousands of other children as well.

In the process of bringing my vision of this Farm to life, I've learned that nothing worthwhile is easy. But if you want it badly enough, and if it's really worth it, you can make a huge impact in your world.

Here are a few things I've learned in the thirteen years it took to create Leg Up Farm. I'm often asked to tell my story, and when I do, I share the following five steps.

1. Have the courage to dream.
2. Visualize your end goal as a reality.
3. Focus on the next step.
4. Do the right things every day.
5. Work at the dream, and never stop believing in what you are doing.

These five steps helped me find my way as I walked an uphill path, with my family by my side. Something wonderful can happen when we pursue a very special dream that is born within our hearts despite the hurdles in our path. When I encountered some of them, it felt like I had hit a brick wall. But I learned that every wall has a top and two sides; I could get around it one way or another. And then there were the smaller hurdles that just bothered me, as if they were mosquitoes buzzing in my ear. I just kept smacking them away!

The most important thing along this journey was finding fellow travelers whom I call angels. The people who helped me didn't necessarily look like angels, and they didn't do anything supernatural, but they came along at the right time and helped me take each next step. If you have a dream, your angels are out there too!

Just as my daughter Brooke inspired me, I hope that someone will inspire you to achieve something unbelievable in your life. Go ahead, start something that makes our world a better place. You'll never regret it — and it will be the greatest journey of your life.

Preface

*"Life isn't about waiting for the storm to pass.
It's about learning to dance in the rain."*

Vivian Greene

On July 29, 1997, my world changed forever. My daughter Brooke was diagnosed with cerebral palsy and developmental delay at the age of one. The diagnosis was later changed to mitochondrial disorder and pervasive developmental disorder in the autism spectrum. Whatever it's called, it is simple for me, as a parent, to describe: our gentle daughter, Brooke, had problems with her muscles and struggled to move her mouth enough to speak. It was also difficult for her to balance enough to walk, and she was easily fatigued. Hearing a diagnosis only confirmed what we had already begun to suspect—that Brooke was going to need a lot of help every day ... forever.

When we first heard the news, I felt a mix of emotions—grief, anger, sadness, and confusion. This kind of news is so hard for a parent to absorb: You don't know what to think. You don't know what to do next. In a way, it's like you're frozen.

When you do finally grasp what this diagnosis means for your child and your family, and have some inkling of how your lives will change, you have to sit with the information for a while. It takes time for you to process it and more time until you realize that you possess the strength to move forward and face the challenges ahead.

When we got to that point, my wife and I pulled ourselves together and asked, "How can we help Brooke?"

As we investigated all local care options, we discovered that there was some care available in our community, but it was scattered and patient-centered in a way that left the rest of the family out. And the main problem was that there was no pediatric therapy facility in our community. At all.

The therapy services we used for Brooke were located miles apart—in opposite directions. There was one heck of a waiting list at every office, and visits there meant paying high deductibles and out-of-pocket costs that piled up quickly. Hardly any of them accepted Medicaid.

Even though the number of children with special needs in our community had increased, several services had recently closed. The bottom line? The care we (and others) needed was not easily accessible.

We quickly realized that Brooke would need something more. We wanted a place for Brooke where families like ours could feel safe—a special place with no barriers, where people could be in community, offering hope and support to one another. This was when our dream of Leg Up Farm was born. Our goal was to give Brooke, and all children, a "leg up" on life, by giving them access to therapy they needed right here in our community.

Our first logo, capturing the magic between Brooke and a horse named Sam, 1998.

Once we identified a need in our community for this kind of organization, it took us 13 years to make Leg Up Farm a reality (longer than I ever could have imagined). Many times we were told, "This sounds amazing …" Too many times, that sentence would continue with, "… but it will never happen." Despite this, we believed every day in our vision of what Leg Up Farm could be, and we were not willing to settle for less.

I had to use every bit of my life experience, learning as I went along, pursuing the dream with the help of my family and countless other angels. I tried to be disciplined and methodical in my approach, attacking one piece of the puzzle at a time. So what if one thing fell through? "Okay," I'd say, "what do we do next?"

At the start, I was working grueling hours in the TV business—doing sales management. I did my best to balance that with being a husband and a busy father of four children. At times I would even have to make business appointments for 5 or 6 a.m. so they wouldn't conflict with family time. We made things work somehow. However, just when I was beginning to get a handle on the chaos in my life, we took another hit.

On February 25, 2008, a few days before her tenth birthday, my youngest daughter, Lauren, was diagnosed with juvenile diabetes. Caring well for one child with special needs was already overwhelming us, and Lauren's illness would be another serious challenge. But there was no time to break down and feel sorry for ourselves, and we persevered as a family. And we continued to believe that if we ever got Leg Up Farm built, life would be better for us and for other families. It would create an oasis of calm where we could spend time together instead of running Brooke—and now Lauren—to various medical care facilities.

Our family difficulties were only the tip of the iceberg; for over a decade, we came up against personal and professional hurdles in pursuing this dream. Eventually, with the help of hundreds of people who came to believe in our Leg Up dream, the Farm opened its doors to the community.

Today, Leg Up Farm is one of the most innovative therapeutic and developmental centers for children in the nation, serving thousands of people. Yet we're not a one-size-fits-all kind of place. Just as our family has many special needs, so do others—so we don't specialize in one specific disability. Leg Up Farm is only specific about this: each child is different and will receive a unique combination of services — from traditional therapies to riding our big black horse, High Boy.

Although the world is full of challenges, all of these fade as families enter our gates. Our Leg Up Farm dream has come true.

When people hear the name Leg Up Farm, many picture our facility as some rickety red barn with a fence in need of repair. I guess that's why most first-time visitors preparing to travel to Leg Up Farm ask me if they will know when they get here.

I laugh and say, "You will know, I promise."

When visitors come around the corner on North Sherman Street, many of them need to pick their jaw up off the steering wheel. Leg Up Farm's expansive, welcoming center is impressive. First, you see a riding stable and an inviting front porch with rocking chairs, where a few parents relax with a good cup of coffee and a favorite book. Then you notice kids climbing all over our colorful playground, ringing chimes, feeding the Koi in our Rainbow Therapy Garden, or petting our donkeys next to the barn. It's a refuge of sorts, a place where kids with disabilities and their families find encouragement, fellowship, and help amid the challenging world in which they find themselves.

When it's time for the children to go back home, they ask their parents when they can come back to Leg Up Farm. They don't fight against going to therapy because they love it. Heck, sometimes our kids don't even realize they are *in* therapy. To most, it feels like they're going to a really fun place to see all their friends!

Parents and siblings who come along enjoy it too. No longer do brothers and sisters have to be bored while sitting in some waiting room — because they *aren't* in a waiting room. They have places they can play, and parents can talk to each other, knowing they all understand what it's like.

This vision and dream has turned out to be attainable, successful, and ultimately replicable. In fact, the radical work we're doing could easily be duplicated over and over across America. I have a new dream that one day, hundreds of thousands of children will benefit from my family's modest dream — all because my little girl named Brooke needed a little extra love and care.

Lauren & Brooke, 2005

1
Cookin' Up Love

"There is no surprise more magical than the surprise of being loved."

Charles Morgan

When I was 15, I saw a vision of beauty standing next to a pile of horse poop.

It was a steaming hot day in July, and instead of babe-watching at the pool, like a typical teenage boy, I was working my summer away at Old Rose Tree Pony Club Camp in south central Pennsylvania as the cook. And standing in front of me was a beautiful girl — the head camp counselor — surrounded by horse manure.

My mom had lined this job up for me because, at the time, I wanted most of all to be a chef. This went way back. I had always enjoyed being in the kitchen. I remember standing on a chair next to my grandmother before I was big enough to see above the counter. I can still smell the pumpkin pie in her oven as if it were baking right now. Grandma took the time to teach me, even though everything took twice as long with me by her side — she was endlessly patient. I was the opposite.

When I first got to camp, I planned the menus, shopped for food, and cleaned the kitchen, which was a mess of cobwebs and dust. Once the kitchen was clean, I should have been perfecting my mac and cheese recipe for the campers. Instead, all I could think about was that cute camp counselor in the barn. Her name was Laurie.

We had chatted by the stable a few times, and one time I had even stolen a kiss. Now I couldn't think of anything besides stealing another one. After dinner one night, I got my chance.

Laurie was hanging around while I was cleaning up the camp kitchen, pretending to read some notices on the wall. I could tell she liked me and was waiting for me, so I quickly finished up. I made a beeline for her and asked if she wanted to go for a walk. She said yes, searching my face and then looking down at my outstretched hand. She took it, and we strolled across one of the fields toward an old stone wall.

We sat on the wall, talking, and watched the sun set as it lit up the clouds with a rosy glow. We ended up sitting there so long the stars came out. It was a magical night and a magical summer. We had so much to say as we got to know each other. The evening walk became a habit, and at every event — swimming, campfires, hikes — the campers saw us side by side.

After we got back from camp, I began to suspect that my mom had set me up with that job just so she could get Laurie and me together. Mom had met Laurie and her mother, Chris, through Pony Club, where for many years my horse-crazy sisters got their fill of riding and showing. It was obvious by Mom's quick approval of anything I wanted to do with Laurie that she thought this was the perfect girl for me.

I found out later that my suspicions were correct. The first time Laurie heard about me was by listening to a phone call between my mom and Chris. Mom reportedly told Chris, "He looks like Sylvester Stallone, and his name is Louie."

Eventually Laurie told me she had been thinking, "He must be a big dork with a name like that!" I guess she got over that, because after we met, she couldn't get enough of me (or at least that's how it seemed). We spent time with each other every chance we could.

After camp ended, we dated for the rest of the summer, but then I began to resent my mom's obvious love for Laurie. It just was not cool in high school to have your mom like your girlfriend that much. It was much more fun being a rebel and dating girls your parents didn't like. Like the high school idiot I was, I ended our romance at the end of the summer, hoping to find some other cute girl to fill the void.

Laurie often reminds me of how I broke her heart that summer. Let me tell you, I have since paid for that mistake many times over! To this day when I ask her to rub my shoulders, she'll give me a look to remind me that there was a time when I didn't realize what I had. She can never pretend to be mad long, though, so we share a laugh, and things are good again.

Laurie and Louie (ages 16 and 15), Summer of 1986.
(Our heads are chopped off — Grandma took this photo.)

I could never find a girl I liked quite as much as Laurie, so even though I saw other girls, I was much more into football that fall than dating. It wasn't just because of my love of the game — it had a great deal to do with my coach.

Coach Cleary was the line coach for our high school football team. An imposing figure built like a power lifter, he wore a blue ball cap at all times. He would stand at the sidelines, shouting words of encouragement, hooting, and hollering. It seemed like he got excited during every game, cheering us on with a big slap on the back when we did even the simplest things the right way! I became the man I am in part because of the man he is and was to me then.

Right after we opened Leg Up Farm, Coach Cleary came to mind. I was reflecting on the influences in my life that helped me to overcome many struggles and challenges over the many years it took to make the dream a reality. During my high school years, he modeled some character traits that I have tried to emulate ever since. From Coach Cleary, I learned the value of encouragement, perseverance and much more. I recently wrote to tell him so.

Dear Coach Cleary:

We often don't know the significance of our actions or the impact we create through our words. As I reflect on this, I wanted you to know how important you were in my life as a coach.

I often hear the words in my head spoken by you like it was yesterday. You said, "Louie is not going to let me down, I know he can do it."

I will always remember your positive nature and the care and concern you had for each of us as players and individuals. I remember the tears in your eyes during our losses and the big smile on your face when we achieved the smallest victory, like a great block or tackle.

Thanks for leading in the trenches with us, for teaching me discipline, for believing in me, and for helping me to see that it is doing the little things — like a good block — that lead to the big wins in life!

- Louie

As I look back, I see four ways Coach Cleary influenced me, and I count those ways as some of the best traits of my adult personality. It wasn't just the words he spoke, although they motivated me to aim higher and reach farther. It also had to do with who Coach Cleary was and what he did.

1. **Work Ethic** - I learned that nothing really worthwhile comes without hard work, so we worked hard. Getting up early and putting in the hours, day after day, all year long, strengthened my muscles. But those hours also strengthened my character. I saw that my size didn't matter nearly as much as the effort I put into practicing. Firsthand, and early in my life, I witnessed that hard work — and discipline — can have a remarkable impact, and I never forgot that.

2. **Self-esteem** - Like most teenagers, I had my share of negative thoughts about myself at times. Coach Cleary's encouraging comments fostered a more positive outlook within me. When he told me to drive through a block during a game, I would make it happen. He encouraged me — and I rose to the occasion, time and again.

3.   **Heart** – I remember watching the rain drip off Coach Cleary's baseball cap and run down the back of his neck. Yet he kept working with us, even after practice was officially finished and he was off the clock. His heart was in it, and he kept drilling us until we pleaded that we were too tired. When things got tough — when it was 40 degrees and pouring down rain — he was still committed to our success. He stayed and gave more of himself. He demonstrated inner strength and taught us how to draw from that to overcome anything we came up against. I learned that when you're on the field and you're hurt and you're losing, you can still find the will to give it everything you have and more. In the end, it is this inner strength that might well cause the big play that changes the course of the game.

4.   **Caring for Others** – Coach Cleary was not only passionate about football, he was passionate about people. He coached our team year-round, working on our endurance and our agility, even though most high school coaches would have stopped after the football season was over. By giving us his time above and beyond what was required, he proved that he cared about us and laid the groundwork for us to go and do likewise in our future vocations.

We all have an impact on each other. Our words and example can be life-giving in ways that inspire and empower others to have the courage to dream — and the tenacity to succeed.

2
Giddy Up, Gal

"Some of us let these great dreams die, but others nourish and protect them; nurse them through bad days till they bring them to the sunshine and light which comes always to those who sincerely hope that their dreams will come true."

Woodrow Wilson

In 1994, I was 23 years old and working on a building project on the property of a family friend. Coincidentally — or not — that family friend was Laurie's mom. I kept my eye out for Laurie, hoping to catch a glimpse of her, and within the first week I got my chance.

One day I had a digging bar in my hand and I saw a beautiful woman walking across the yard to the barn in a raggedy old grey sweatshirt and a pair of shorts. I could see a lot of leg — and her mucking shoes. I quickly realized it was Laurie from my camp days back in 1986. The emotions from our summer together returned and hit me like a brick. I remember at that moment thinking, *"I have to marry that woman."*

When I saw her, I could once again smell the scent of her hair when it brushed against my face as she squeezed me tightly on that old stone wall as kids. However, that was a long time ago, and our lives had changed.

After our summer together, Laurie and I had dated many other people and had other relationships. I was now the father of Olivia, my silly brown-eyed girl who was born dancing and singing and has never stopped.

When I met Laurie again, Olivia was three years old, and Laurie had a two-year-old named Toby, who was already starting to read. Unfortunately, neither of our relationships had worked out, and we were both single parents. Laurie and I were now caring for our toddlers full-time…and we were both unattached.

This was when our mothers got involved—clearly, again, they knew something we didn't. Laurie's mom Chris called me on the phone one day, asking if I could build some fence on her farm. I said yes, unaware of her ulterior motives.

This turned out to be a very difficult job. The section of fence she asked me to build was just below her barn, and would cover only about 80 feet, but I swear, half of the ten holes I had to dig were straight through rock. I had to chip away at the rock in order to break it up, because the holes needed to be a full three feet deep to set the posts.

I remember immediately thinking this job was horrible. After just an hour, my hands were numb from striking the rock with that long, steel digging bar. But then, *zing!* All that pain disappeared the moment I saw Laurie. All of a sudden I didn't want the job to end.

That night I asked my mom to find out what was going on with Laurie. Did she have someone in her life? Laurie later told me she had wondered the same thing when she ran into me.

As soon as I got the word back that Laurie wasn't seeing anyone, I asked her out and we began dating again. We jumped into a relationship head first, not realizing what we were doing—instead, we let our hearts and passion for each other steer our path.

On our first date overlooking the amusement park at Hershey, we talked for hours, filling in the gaps since we'd been apart and reminiscing about the past. I found I appreciated Laurie's values and the type of person she was now more than ever. Our personal lives were definitely more complicated, but the feelings returned as if we had never been apart.

We spent many evenings together, discussing a possible shared future—but one that now included jobs and kids. I found time to be with Laurie whenever I had a moment. Sleep didn't matter, because I was running on love. Our future was going to be perfect! We would get married, buy a house, and join our families.

We could see everything as we dreamed together: a house with a little yard and a swing set where our children would play. We would sit around the dinner table, laughing together and sharing the day's events. We would start new traditions at holidays and carry on the ones from each of our families. There might be a tough time or two, but the sheer excitement of this fresh new relationship dwarfed that notion, and all we could see were the good times we would have. I wish I could have one of those nights back again—before we knew how difficult life could become.

I proposed to Laurie using a 30-second television commercial. Because of my job, it made perfect sense. The only catch was that she had to be watching TV at the exact moment the commercial would run. As I turned the channel away from the 1995 Super Bowl pre-game, Laurie was confused, because she knew I loved football. She scrutinized my face, but I just smiled as if I had nothing up my sleeve.

The next thing Laurie knew, familiar photographs appeared on the TV set. Images of both of us as babies and at camp, holding hands, flitted across the screen. Then I was on camera, standing in a field where we wanted to build a home, proposing. Laurie, surprised and amazed, turned to me and answered, "Yes!" No cameras or lights were there that day, but that moment is one we will never forget.

Louie & Laurie, January 1995.

3
Too Close to Home?

*"We are each of us angels with only one wing,
and we can only fly by embracing one another."*

Luciano de Crescenzo

If Laurie's life had been busy when I met her, she was about to watch her busy schedule practically launch into orbit. She was an athletic trainer at the local high school, helping students prepare for a variety of sports and standing by during games in case of the odd sprained ankle or muscle cramp. That meant her hours varied, to put it mildly. She was also a horse trainer for dressage, a competitive equine sport that's a little like horse ballet. She'd work with her horses on their stamina, athleticism and specific gaits to get ready for horse shows that took up most weekends from May through September. She loved working with the horses so much you couldn't call it a second job, but it did take up a lot of time.

Not only was Laurie working more than 40 hours per week and grooming the horses, she was taking care of her son Toby and dating me. Oh, and in her "spare time" she was planning our wedding. The big day was in May.

One Tuesday in April, I drove to Laurie's place after work. Laurie's mother Chris had come over to give Toby a bath. Because Laurie lived in the in-law quarters that went with Chris's ranch house, she didn't have to go far to visit or help out.

That spring evening, Chris and I were talking while Laurie finished taking care of the horses. Laurie had been late coming home from a track meet and was still outside. I spoke to my future mother-in-law about our wedding, which would happen in a few weeks, and about where Laurie and I were planning to live after that.

Chris brought up the topic Laurie and I had been dancing around since we'd gotten engaged. "I can't see Laurie driving over here every morning and night to take care of the horses," she observed. "You've seen it. She doesn't even get home until 10:00 some nights, and then she has to go out there for another hour. Now that she'll have two kids in the house…" Chris trailed off.

"I know," I agreed. "But what can we do if the zoning board won't cooperate?" We'd been hoping to build on Chris's property, but that was a no-go, so we were checking out other properties nearby.

"We're still looking," I reminded Chris, "*and running out of time,*" I thought, shaking my head.

Chris looked down at her hands, still warm from Toby's bathwater. We knew Laurie needed to be close to her horses, because training and caring for them was a seven-day-a-week job. Any midnight thunderstorms also meant running out to bring the horses into the barn.

But it was more than that. I saw how much she loved just being with the horses. It calmed her, and the routine helped her shake off any problems that had come up during the day. "We have to be nearby," I agreed. "It will work out somehow."

Chris responded with a crooked smile. "I guess Laurie will always have horse fever," she said. "She got it before she could walk. I remember her crawling under a neighbor's fence to get to their horses. Every weekend she would beg us to take her to a ranch a few miles away so she could give the horses treats." She was quiet for a minute, reminiscing, then spoke up again. "She would giggle when the horses' whiskers tickled her hand."

Chris got up, peeked in on Toby, and came back to her chair at the table. "I can still see Laurie's face on her seventh birthday when I surprised her with her first pony, Sam. Small as she was, I thought she was going to knock me down when she ran up to hug me!"

Laurie still had Sam, though he was getting on in years now. By the time I came back on the scene, there were four others in the barn: Tauney, Jazz, Vinnie, and Chippie, Laurie's prize competition horse. They were more like lifelong companions than pets, and I couldn't see her ever giving any of them up.

Laurie came in suddenly, bringing a blast of cold air in with her. She closed the door, stomping her boots, then peeling them off on the mat. She was flushed with the cold but her face was radiant. Catching my eye, she came over and kissed me, then went to hug her mom.

As we paused in our conversation, Laurie grabbed a Dove chocolate out of the kitchen cabinet, eating it quickly. We watched, amused, knowing it was her nightly ritual after her barn chores.

"Come here, babe," I offered, patting my leg.

She smiled and shook her head, protesting, "I'm filthy and I smell like a barn!" and pulled a chair up close to mine.

Chris and I looked at each other and then at Laurie. As if by silent agreement, we brought the subject up. "We were just talking about how we could keep you close to the horses," I ventured.

Laurie looked from one of us to the other. She raised her eyebrows. "Any ideas?"

Chris hesitated, then spoke. "I do have an idea, but I don't know what you two would think."

"What is it?" Laurie asked, brightening. I looked at Chris questioningly.

"What if we switched?" she suggested. We must have looked puzzled, because she continued.

"What if you two moved to my house..." She waited a beat, adding "and I moved here?"

The question hung in the air. *Hmmm*, I thought. *That's interesting. I'd be living fifty yards from my mother-in-law. Good thing we get along.*

A series of emotions flitted across Laurie's face. One looked a lot like hope. I could see her trying to gauge my reaction. "Honey, I know you wanted to build our own place. What do you think?"

I got up and walked over to the window. I was throwing the idea around in my mind, holding it up to the light to see if it had any holes. Sure, it would be less grand than the house I'd imagined building.

But it would work for the horses, and it would be nice for the kids to grow up next door to their Grammy.

Both women were watching me. I shrugged. "I'm thinking, I'm thinking!" I joked. They laughed, and some of the tension left the room.

As we talked about it, the idea grew. The more we went over how things might work, the more it made sense. By the time Chris walked back to the ranch house, Laurie and I were talking like it could actually happen. It wasn't quite ready for our family because we were going to need more space. We began throwing ideas around about how we could add on to the ranch house if we decided to live there.

"How many bedrooms do you think we'll need?" I asked Laurie, winking pointedly to make her blush. She chuckled, shaking her head, and we kept talking as we figured it out together: Did we need a bigger kitchen, a more spacious living room or more bathrooms for all of our kids? Could we really make this work?

Planning for a move like this was starting to feel a lot like fun (for me, it was way more fun than choosing my groom's outfit, which I pretty much delegated to Laurie).

I started drafting up a rough design for the enlarged home. When the idea of a log home came up, I started to get excited. We both loved the look and feel of a log home and we could see how a rustic-looking addition would fit into the style of the house and tie it in with the look of the barn.

After a few days of calling each other to discuss how we wanted the new addition to look, I drove up to meet Laurie for lunch. We looked at some pictures Laurie had cut out of a magazine and decided on a light pine stain for the logs with a hand-hewn exterior and smooth interior finish so the kids wouldn't get splinters. We looked at each other and said, "Let's do it."

We were married on May 27, 1995, with our toddlers by our side. Toby was three, and Olivia was four. I notified the post office and my boss of my new address, and our blended family adventure began.

Off to our honeymoon in a horse-drawn carriage.

4
Small Miracles

"Small steps result in small miracles."

Megan Giordano, Leg Up Farm Staff Member

Difficult is not a strong enough word to describe the first few years of our marriage. *Insane* is more accurate.

One month into our marriage, we found out that Laurie was pregnant. We were overjoyed, but concerned, as her schedule was already tight, and a new baby, while wonderful, would put her commitments over the top.

Meanwhile, Chris told us to go ahead with construction while she stayed in the ranch house which, she pointed out, would be easier on Toby and Olivia. We knew she was right, so we accepted.

My new mother-in-law was a trooper, packing and cooking and sleeping amid the clutter while we tore a wall down and stripped off old paneling. The sound of circular saws at 6 a.m. might awaken her some days, but she took it all in stride. What could have been a horrible time ended up helping us to bond. The three of us adults joked about the sawdust and the noise, reminding each other it would look great—eventually. We ate together often, doing the cooking at our place when Chris' kitchen was out of commission. For all the kids knew, we had two homes. It was like going back in time, when several generations would live together on a farm.

Still, Laurie's place was so small that we were *absolutely* ready to switch homes after the construction was over, and I'm sure Chris was ready for some quiet. By November, our addition was finally complete and the move began.

I didn't have a ton of things, but I made sure I brought with me the poster bed that had been mine when I was a boy, which had belonged to my mother and her father before that. We placed it in Olivia's room, covering it with a pink and blue Amish quilt. We moved Toby's bunk bed down the hall into a room that was soon overflowing with stuffed animals. Last, we began to set up the nursery for our new addition to the family, Brooke, with a pink wind-up horse that played *Twinkle, Twinkle Little Star*. We were home at last.

Both of us were working full-time, and we often felt stretched thin as we tried to get settled into the new place, take care of the farm as well as two small children, and prepare for the one on the way. One more complicating factor: we had two sets of step-parents to deal with outside of our home.

This made planning holidays and birthdays difficult, but managing even our daily schedules was becoming overwhelming. We didn't always agree on how to plan for Olivia and Toby to have time with their other parents, but eventually we all learned to work together, most of the time.

The dreams we had carefully built changed quickly, and our life became ridiculously hard — fast. We went through the motions of caring for our children, but, really, most of the time we were in survival mode. It took everything we had to manage our home and family. We began to consider how we could handle everything, especially after Brooke arrived. We asked ourselves, *Could — and should — Laurie leave her job?*

Laurie loved her work, and if she left her job, it would be tough to get re-certified as an athletic trainer, if she wanted to go back to the same career.

Yet for Laurie and for me, this seemed like the only option. We didn't want to put the kids in daycare or ask Laurie's mom to watch them all the time, and I had to keep my job, which was paying most of the bills.

Laurie's pregnancy was advancing quickly, and soon we were in delivery mode. Brooke was born on February 13, 1996, and despite our best efforts, her entry into this world was grueling.

Laurie's labor was one of the most intense things I have ever experienced in my life, and that is only a fraction of what it was for Laurie. I'll spare you most of the details, but it was tough for many reasons. The labor took over 18 hours, Brooke was facing backwards, and the umbilical cord was wrapped around her neck. I've never seen a doctor move that fast. We were terrified.

Finally, after all the panic and pain, we had a new baby girl, our first child together. We were thrilled—even though Brooke's first habit was projectile vomiting. The doctors told us not to worry, because her weight and growth were right where they needed to be.

There are moments when I beat myself up for not pushing the doctors harder or looking further into Brooke's symptoms. Today, I would have questioned the reflux and certain milestones, because I am better educated, but how could I have known? I have met many parents since then who had found themselves in this same situation. They wonder too how they could have missed the signs.

I don't know if a difficult birth has any connection with Brooke's symptoms, but I do know that it took every ounce of Laurie's will to deliver Brooke into this world. With her birth behind us, we heaved a big sigh of relief, thinking the hardest part was over.

Once Brooke was born, Laurie could no longer resist the pull to stay at home. At the end of the football season, in November 1996, Laurie turned in her notice. When she arrived home from her last day of work, she told me, "I'm finally where my heart wants to be." Looking more relaxed than she had in months, she began to focus all of her energy, emotion, and will on our kids.

We all still live on this beautiful farm together. It's been 18 years now, and we don't have any plans to move. Laurie still has her mom next door. She can see her horses from the kitchen window, and we have a beautiful place where our children have now grown up and made their parents proud.

Toby & Olivia, 1995.

5
I Will Survive!

"Going in one more round when you don't think you can — that's what makes all the difference in your life."

Rocky Balboa (from *Rocky IV*)

Although he bragged about the strength of his abs, Houdini died from a punch in the gut (his appendix ruptured). You never know when you will take that blow that brings you to your knees. For me, the date was July 29, 1997, when, at 17 months of age, Brooke was diagnosed with cerebral palsy and developmental delay.

We had been to see a developmental pediatrician at a children's hospital in Baltimore because things just didn't seem right with Brooke. Her pediatrician had continually told us she was a "late bloomer," but as parents, we knew something was off.

I will never forget that day at the specialist's office, feeling like my world was crumbling. They gave us the diagnosis, and just like that, our appointment was over. We stood, dazed, just outside the exam room in a hallway wallpapered in pastel stripes and balloons. I resented this generic attempt at cheerfulness: it felt out of place in an office where you could be given such awful news.

Leaning against the wall, I put my arm around Laurie, who had begun to cry. For the first time, I didn't know what to say to her. I tried to tell her it would be okay, but I really didn't know if it would be.

I attempted to play out Brooke's entire life in my head. Would she ever drive a car? Would she go to school…and read and write? And then there were dreams—hers and mine: Would I get to walk her down the aisle, and would she someday have a little house with children of her own playing in the yard?

The specialists told us that Brooke would need constant care. So a more haunting question arose: who would take care of her when we were no longer around? We realized this question would never fade.

I was sad…and heartbroken.

I didn't understand the words "cerebral palsy" and "developmental delay." All I had known up to this point was that Brooke wasn't doing some of the things she should have been doing at her age. Maybe she could still be a "late bloomer." I wondered what it all meant, and it made my palms sweat and the back of my neck twitch. Stress, I thought, recognizing the signs. *Big time.*

The evaluation they handed us was full of complex, confusing concepts—concepts foreign to young parents. What in the world were "significant global developmental delays", "neuro-motor abnormalities", "lower extremity tone", and "pathologic reflexes"? I could hardly make myself say these words out loud—and I thought if I didn't, maybe the diagnosis wouldn't become real.

There was bad news about Brooke's developmental function, too. Although she was a year-and-a-half old by then, her motor skills were those of a nine-month-old. Her cognition was behind, and her visual and motor skills were those of a baby under a year old. It was as if some trigger had been switched and Brooke had stopped developing at 10 months.

I was in denial. I wanted the doctors to be wrong. I tried to convince myself that, just maybe, Brooke would catch up, and we would never have to go back to that wallpapered office again.

After the diagnosis that day, a medical assistant came out of another door and led us down the striped hallway so another person in cheery scrubs could explain our discharge instructions. Laurie was pregnant with Lauren at the time, and they asked us if we wanted to run some genetic testing.

I was proud of Laurie's quick response. "It won't make a difference in our decision, so why do it?" she said. I agreed, and a note was put in our small file. That file would grow…quickly.

We felt like our hearts had just gone through a meat grinder. We took Brooke home, fed everyone dinner, and tried to sleep, our dreams full of falling off cliffs or running away from pursuers. We awoke, unrefreshed and apprehensive, sensing we were about to switch into high gear again.

Immediately, a whirlwind of doctors and confusion swirled in our lives. Recommendations for "follow-ups" about Brooke's evaluation. Recommendations for physical therapy. A pediatric orthopedics consult. Speech therapy. More special instructions. A brain MRI and chromosomal work-up. We were overwhelmed.

Little did we know that our routine of doctor visits and search for answers had just begun. On June 12, 1998, following dozens of appointments and multiple blood tests—and less than a year after receiving our first punch in the gut—Brooke's diagnosis was changed.

It was now official: Brooke had a mitochondrial disorder and pervasive developmental disorder. In other words, she had autism and a cell disease that could wreak havoc with just about any body system. Once again we were confused. We didn't understand these new big words and how they would impact our lives. But mostly we hoped there was a cure that could make it all go away.

By the time we had a handle on Brooke's diagnosis, our youngest daughter, Lauren, had been born and was three months old. We had learned that mitochondrial disorder was genetic and could appear in any of our children. Still reeling from this news, we began to worry about Lauren. Would it affect her?

We had her tested and, sure enough, she had the same underlying mitochondrial disorder. To prevent any cellular damage, she was put on a liquid vitamin cocktail at three months old. This seemed to jump-start her growth; she was walking at just seven months and climbing on the counter by her first birthday.

It was difficult to watch her and Brooke, who needed our attention because she couldn't take care of herself, even as she grew up. We still had to do the same things we had done for her when she was a baby—bathing her, feeding her, getting her dressed. Most children can start to do these things for themselves. For a child with special needs, advances can be slow…or never come.

In the midst of this, we were married and trying to be a couple, which is hard enough without extra stress in your life. Sometimes I got anxious because I couldn't see that next moment of intimacy with Laurie—those times when we could just be a couple. I loved being with her, and the times when we could share a laugh or kiss by ourselves were precious snapshots in time. It felt like there were never enough of them.

Laurie was, and is, incredible. She's the kind of mother who feels everything her family feels. Like many moms, she is continually multitasking. But the recent problems, along with normal new-baby routines, had her physically, emotionally and mentally beat. As for me, I did my best to be supportive, but it was never enough.

At the same time, I was angry for Brooke. I was mourning the loss of all the special moments she would never experience. I was her dad. I wanted to fix what was wrong. My heart sank when I thought of the moments Laurie and I wouldn't be able to share with Brooke—simple things like science fairs and talent shows. And I felt guilty about the time we didn't have left over to give to our other children, Olivia, Toby, and Lauren, while we were caring for Brooke.

During this difficult time, Laurie and I had nothing left at the end of the day. We would simply manage to survive, dropping from exhaustion onto our pillows at night, only to rise the next day with the sun, ready to face it all over again with whatever smile we could muster. We knew what we were doing was important even if it meant sacrificing career advancement, weekends away, and other interests and hobbies. We knew that we were somehow *called* to do this, to give our *special* family special care, and we rose to meet the call. We persevered when that was all we could do, and it was enough.

6
Can We Go Yet?

*"When life gives you lemons, you don't make lemonade.
You use the seeds to plant a whole orchard - an entire franchise!"*

Anthon St. Maarten

As we stepped into the elevator at a children's hospital in Baltimore, another mom followed us. She cradled her little girl on her hip. The girl was about six.

They were very quiet. They seemed used to being at the hospital; they took their time getting into the elevator and automatically pushed the button for the fourth floor.

When I looked at the little girl, I saw that she was very pale, as if she hadn't spent much time outside. She wore a paisley bandana; under it you could see that she had lost all of her hair.

In the midst of our own crisis, our hearts went out to that little girl. We felt the desire to help her—even though we were falling apart at the seams in our own lives. That mom might not know whether her child would make it through the week. It made us reassess our situation and be grateful again for what we *could* be thankful for.

It's usually pretty quiet in hospital pediatric waiting rooms. So when your kids—the ones who aren't there to see the doctor—get loud, you shush them. When they ask how much longer, you tell them 15 minutes. Next thing you know it's been 3 hours. Meanwhile you've been waiting forever for an MRI, for test results, or just for the doctor to fit you in.

Sometimes you're in a room with other families who have kids with ongoing medical conditions, and you find yourself comparing your situation with theirs—not a good thing, let me tell you. You either wind up feeling sorry for yourself or bad because their situation is so much worse, like the little girl with the bandana. And it's no picnic for siblings, either.

People stare. They don't understand why your child is lying on the floor. Sometimes people frowned at our kids, assuming we weren't able to discipline them. But the truth was, sometimes Brooke was on the floor because her legs were fatigued from trying to walk…and she couldn't walk anymore. Sometimes our other kids started lying on the floor as well, coloring or reading, because they'd been there for hours. They were cranky, and rightly so. Who wants to spend all their time at a medical facility?

Even worse, you've just dragged your kids away from something they wanted to do to head to yet another doctor's appointment. I'm sure Olivia would have been happier back in our kitchen making crafts out of buttons. And Toby? He would rather have been playing basketball with the kids in the neighborhood. We felt bad about it, but there was nothing we could do.

By the time we were on our way home from these visits, we were usually starving, and Laurie and I were always disappointed — again. No better prognosis. No magic cure. Just a long, cranky ride home.

On top of waiting for all the blood tests, sleep studies and orthopedic visits for splints for Brooke's feet, we were constantly making our other kids sacrifice their own interests. Off we all went, to the acupuncturist, the naturopath, the chiropractor, or the latest wonder-working massage therapist. And of course all of this cost money! It meant thousands of dollars in uncovered medical expenses — money we would surely rather have spent on something our whole family could enjoy. But we kept trying anything and everything, hoping something would help our little girl.

We began to realize it would make a lot more sense if we didn't have to go to so many different appointments. If the specialists Brooke needed were in the same building, we wouldn't spend so much time driving around and waiting. And why was there rarely anything for our other kids to do while we all waited for Brooke?

Other families who had children with special needs were jumping through these same hoops. They were just as tired as we were. They wished there was another option too. A thought began to form in my head that wouldn't go away: *what if there was a place for everyone like us — an inviting place where we actually all wanted to go?*

7
Question Everything

*"Life is filled with unanswered questions,
but it is the courage to seek those answers
that continues to give meaning to life."*

J.D. Stroube

During all the chaos in my family's life, a question I had asked Laurie back in February 1997 went unanswered. Brooke hadn't been diagnosed yet; she had just turned one, and we were busy with a million things. I asked, "What would you think about starting a therapeutic horseback riding program at our house on the weekends?"

I had butterflies in my stomach as I asked again, less timidly this time. It was a big question. I had gone back and forth, even before we knew about Brooke: If we did it, it would take a lot of time. But it could help a lot of kids, and starting a therapeutic riding program made perfect sense to me. And it could mean we wouldn't have to drive Brooke around as much anymore. Laurie was a horse trainer — and she was an athletic trainer. She was great with kids…and horses. We had horses at our home, and I had grown up with horses. It seemed like a natural fit for our family because it combined something that we knew and loved with a way to help others.

I understood the healing relationship that happened between horses and humans, and I had heard about horses helping children with physical or behavioral issues. I had seen for myself the way a kid's face would light up around our horses, and I knew what a stress reliever it was for Laurie. She loved their companionship, claiming they always listened when she talked to them and sent her subtle cues of their affection that felt a lot like friendship. I had watched Laurie communicate wordlessly with these gentle giants. It was almost as if a secret language of unconditional love flowed between them. It was mystical.

But this was still a crazy idea in many ways — we were barely getting through each day as it was. So when I asked that question of Laurie about riding therapy — I wasn't sure what she would say.

Since we had been engaged, I'd been in the habit of thinking up big ideas and bouncing them off Laurie. One time I suggested, "Let's start a vineyard." "Sure," was Laurie's answer. She is always up for whatever I want to do, no matter how weird it sounds. (I love that about her.)

 One short month after we got married, I declared one day, "I want to be an organic farmer." She didn't bat an eyelash, and just said, "Cool."

A few weeks later, I had a new idea: "Let's open a restaurant," and Laurie simply replied, "Go ahead and do it."

It was as if she believed each adventure was possible and knew I could do it if I set my mind to it. Of course, she probably knew most of these ideas wouldn't happen, but she was willing to let me dream. I think she would have gone along with any of my ideas, but I'm not sure she realized I was serious when I blurted out this latest one.

I repeated again, phrasing the question as a suggestion, "Come on, let's start a therapeutic riding program." It was just after dinner, and we were in the living room, picking up the toys Olivia and Toby had left lying around.

"I guess we could," Laurie offered, shrugging.

"I mean it, let's really do it. For real." I stepped closer and tilted her chin up so I could see her expression. "Okay?"

Laurie was silent, considering the idea, then gestured for me to follow her outside. Striding over to two of the horses standing at the fence, she was quiet. I could practically see the wheels turning.

"We have enough space…" she murmured, "but we'd have to get some gentler horses…" She spun in a circle, surveying the farm and the barn. Finally she seemed to come to a decision. She turned to me and said, "Okay."

"Okay? Really?" I asked, my eyes big with hope. She nodded. I threw my arms around her and swung her in a circle.

"Yes, okay! Really!" she said, laughing.

Now that Laurie had given me the green light, the question began to dominate my thoughts. I became what you might call obsessed — something that had happened to me years ago with another question.

"Can I have a go cart? Pleeeease?" This was a question I must have asked my parents dozens of times the year I was 11.

They were used to questions from me, and often joked that I would never run out of them. I was forever badgering them with "Why?" and "Why not?" and "How?" They were pretty patient with me, even when I took our radio apart to see how it worked.

But the question that kept coming back that particular year was about a go-cart. I wanted one—in a *big* way. I was dreaming of chrome wheels, but what was most important to me was speed. I wanted a go-cart that was really fast, like the one my buddy down the street had. Or maybe even faster. I pictured zooming down the back alley behind our house and skidding through the mud. I talked about that go-cart all the time.

By May I still didn't have one, but I was determined to get one before summer started. To get ready to work on it, I spent a lot of time with my grandfather, who loved to tinker. He began to teach me how to repair things, and I soaked it all up, knowing it would come in handy when I got that go-cart.

When we moved back from Penn State where my dad was getting his degree, we moved into the apartment upstairs from Paw Paw's business, an insurance company. It was great for us kids to be nearby, because we loved spending time with him and Grandma.

Paw Paw was tall and thin, with large, dark-framed glasses. He was a quiet, spiritual man, but when he spoke it was powerful. He often took me to men's retreats and bible studies early on Saturday mornings. I remember the men laughing at how many pancakes such a little boy could eat!

Paw Paw was patient with me no matter what we were doing. When I was four, he helped me connect the tracks on my toy train set the right way so it wouldn't keep crashing off the tracks. When he taught me how to cut the grass, he walked next to me every step as I pushed the mower. It probably took an extra hour, but he never complained.

Paw Paw let me fiddle around with the tools in his basement workshop, where I learned to make things. I would make gifts for our relatives — things I'm pretty sure they had little use for but for which I received many thank you's. He had given me a wood-burning kit when I was 8, and I loved to burn my name into everything I made.

Paw Paw taught me about work, but he also showed me how he cared for his customers. I recalled the stories of his customers when we worked to open Leg Up Farm. Through his teaching and my own career, I realized that the way staff members treat people makes all the difference.

Paw Paw's support also helped me learn the all-important lesson of perseverance. I watched how he lived and was inspired to always try to finish what I started.

This was important over the 13 years we built Leg Up Farm, but it was also very important the spring when I was 11, and doing anything possible to get that go-cart.

One day I spotted a go-cart for sale in someone's yard on the way to my grandparents' house. The sign on it said $75. It was old, and most of its parts were disassembled and jammed into a cardboard box next to the sign. It didn't even have a seat, but that didn't matter. I wanted that go-cart!

For months, I had been mowing the lawn at Paw Paw's business and saving my money. On the way home, I would walk to the bank to deposit the three dollars I had earned.

My parents said no. It was too dangerous, they told me. Determined, I added up my allowance and the money in my bank account and saw I'd have enough in a few weeks. I kept pleading my case, and my parents finally let me buy the go-cart—I think they thought it would never run.

I asked Mr. Keeney, Paw Paw's neighbor who repaired lawn mowers, for a quick weld or advice on how to make the engine work. He was glad to help.

My grandmother helped me out with the go-cart by teaching me how to sew to make a seat for it. She took me to a fabric store where three little old ladies worked at a big counter with a measuring tape on it. Grandma helped me find the perfect fabric—sturdy imitation black leather. For two solid days, we worked together in her laundry room as she showed me how to make a pattern from the seat and how to turn the material inside-out before you sewed it, so you'd end up with a nice seam when you stuffed it with foam. I tore the paper pattern a few times, but she would just laugh and help me start over.

Grandma patiently guided my hands as I tried to thread her sewing machine, weaving the string through the confusing path of ups and downs, and finally through the tiny hole in the needle. We stuffed the seat pad, sewed it tightly, and were ready to put it on the cart. Working together, we attached the seat to the frame, with a little help from Paw Paw. After that was done, I painted the go-cart, fixed the chain, and put it all together. Finally, it was complete. Much to my parents' chagrin, by the end of the summer, I had a metallic blue go-cart with a shiny black seat that I raced around the yard.

Isn't she a beauty?

I didn't know it then, but every bit of that willingness to believe, and every ounce of strength and patience I had learned from tinkering on that broken-down old go-cart, would emerge again in the planning phase of Leg Up Farm. My family and I would be pushed to the limit as we labored to bring Leg Up Farm to life. But I kept the final vision in mind: instead of a shiny blue go-cart, the dream was now a place where kids could go to become well again.

8
The Courage to Dream

"When one has a vision and is passionate about making it a reality, unbelievable things happen."

      David Skerpon, Capital Blue Cross
      (about Leg Up Farm)

I wasn't your average football player. At barely 150 lbs. and not quite 5'6", I was easily the smallest guy on the team. I played quarterback in tenth grade, but I had one problem: I couldn't see over the linemen to throw passes. Nevertheless, encouraged by Dr. Thompson, our District Superintendent, I started every game on offense as well as defense and played on every special team.

Dr. Thompson, or Dr. T, as we called him, came every morning to lift weights with us at the high school. And when I say in the morning, I'm talking four a.m., during the school year and all summer long. Let me tell you, it was really cold at four a.m. in the winter—and really awful getting up that early in the summer when all of your friends were sleeping until noon. There were very few people in that weight room before the sun rose. But Dr. Thompson was there. He used this time to talk to those of us who showed up about things we were facing, whether someone's parents were divorcing…or one of us was just trying to grow a beard.

He also kept us accountable with our education, checking with our teachers on our grades and making sure we were showing up for class. I guess that's how he knew when we were struggling with a certain subject or when we weren't giving it our all. He made sure to make himself heard if there was a problem.

He taught us in the best way possible; sharing stories from his own life. Among other things, Dr. T had been in the Army Special Forces, stationed in Vietnam. During one explosion, he was badly burned and hid in a rice paddy. Hours later he was found — fortunately by our own troops. We hung on every word he said as he explained all of the details.

From his stories and the fact that he showed up every morning without fail, we learned about discipline, courage, and perseverance. No matter what challenge I took on, he would always tell me, "Louie, you can do it!"

As Dr. T encouraged me, my size began to matter less. I switched to Running Back on offense, and Outside Linebacker on defense. I practiced harder. I worked harder. I played with heart, giving everything I had on every play. Pretty soon I could knock down guys twice my size, and in my senior year, I was named co-captain of the team.

Dr. Thompson taught me to lead with my heart, be disciplined, try to work harder than anyone else, and never give up. I have had to return to these basics time and again as we have worked to make Leg Up Farm a reality.

9
Visualize Your End Goal As Reality

"Every day you see the kids coming in the door and you see them making progress and leave laughing. It's a great feeling to go home every night and feel like you've made a difference."

Tom O'Connor, Leg Up Farm Staff Member

Lauren had a connection with her older sister, Brooke, that no one else had. Even as a toddler she was able to engage Brooke in a way we couldn't. Brooke's therapists picked up on this, so they would include Lauren in the sessions. To work on Brooke's coordination, they would give a ball to Lauren to throw to Brooke, and because it was her little sister throwing it, Brooke would try really hard to catch it.

The first time we noticed our daughters' special connection, Lauren was only four months old. She had been experimenting with the word "Da da," which we thought was pretty advanced for her age, but that was about all she'd said. One Saturday morning Laurie and I were trying to get Brooke, who was then two years old, to talk. We had the video camera on and were about to put it away, so we kept saying, "Goodbye." All of a sudden Lauren piped up: "Goodbye." We were so surprised, and even Brooke noticed. From then on, they were partners.

Brooke's sessions were always difficult for her, but to Lauren, they were just fun. Pretty early on, she sensed she was helping Brooke, and, to this day, that sense has never faded.

As they grew up together, Lauren was never one to let Brooke get away with anything. If someone asked Brooke to get her book bag and she didn't do it, that person might go and get the bag for her. Not Lauren. She knew what Brooke could do, and she would call her out on it, treating her like anyone else and expecting her to do her part. Because she knew that Lauren wouldn't do it for her, Brooke rose to the occasion and did things for herself. Seeing Brooke through Lauren's eyes helped us focus on her abilities—rather than her disabilities.

This approach is what we were trying to do with Leg Up Farm. I sat down with a few people who believed in the dream, and we came up with a vision statement we were determined to carry out:

Create the ultimate therapy center for children with special needs and their families by bringing everything together under one roof in the most amazing, engaging, child-friendly environment possible. Therapists, family, teachers and volunteers will work as a team, enabling everyone to share ideas that will ultimately benefit the children they assist.

To show how it would work, we created a visual version. We placed children in the middle of the picture, because everything we would do would be about the kids. We surrounded them with the other pieces of the puzzle we'd need, and we encircled it with a border representing everyone in the community who would help.

Having such a place would be awesome. We weren't sure what to call it or even what type of center it would be. Basically, we wanted to drop a medical facility into a farm setting. There was no category for that. I knew we wanted to start with therapeutic riding, so as I thought about this, a picture came into my head—one of someone helping a child climb onto a horse—we call that giving someone a "leg up". That was it! There was our name: Leg Up Farm.

In November 1997, we filed the articles of incorporation and immediately got to work on qualifying as a non-profit. In May 1998, we were official: Leg Up Farm was an entity.

Hurdle #1: Complete.

Before we had a Board of Directors, before we had done any real fundraising or in-depth research and before we had an office, Laurie and I contributed more than $8,000 out of our own pocket to move Leg Up Farm forward. But we couldn't keep that up — now that Laurie wasn't working and my attention was split between my "real job" and the work on Leg Up Farm, money wasn't exactly rolling into our household.

Most people would have been reluctant to see their income drop and their spouse obsessed with a dream that took almost all of their free time. But Laurie wasn't like that. She believed in giving, and she trusted me with our finances. Even when things got a little tight and money was going out to pay for something for the Farm, Laurie knew it would also eventually benefit our family, and other families like ours. Still, in order to move forward we had to have significant investment from outside — we didn't have any more to give.

Before our dream could become a reality, there would be many times when our venture would run out of money. In November 1999, we were close to the edge: we had $25.74 in the company account. I just had to gather my courage, pick up the phone, and ask for help.

In one case, our architect completed a significant amount of work without having the money. Others would often agree to accept just a few hundred dollars a month, along with a personal IOU. Some even reduced their bills. It was as if they wanted to believe in the dream too. Their support meant more to me than just a donation. It meant that what we were doing was important, that there needed to be a place like Leg Up Farm, and that we needed to keep on going. Leg Up Farm became bigger as it became more than just our dream. The generosity of spirit of a growing number of supporters who walked alongside us gave us momentum and strength.

We had an architect draw what our vision of Leg Up Farm would look like, and we all fell in love with his interpretation of our dream.

"A Very Inviting Place" by Seth Harry, 1999.

In order to bring our dream to life, I realized we would have to roll out Leg Up Farm very gradually, although I wanted all of it *now*. We came up with three Phases of development.

During Phase One we would build riding stables and an arena, a main therapy building, a therapy pool, and outdoor play spaces. During Phase Two, we would construct a lodging facility with a bed and breakfast feel, as well as a restaurant. Finally, in Phase Three, we would build an assisted living facility, doctors' offices, and an organic marketplace where disabled adults could sell items grown and made on the Farm.

Sound ambitious? You bet!

I was too excited to be realistic. In my mind, we would set up our office, find some land, and just start building. No problem, right? I thought we could be open to serve children no later than 2004. This was all while I was working a full-time position in television advertising an hour away.

Hope dies hard, so believe it or not, I set the target dates as if we could do it all in one year. Um…okay, I was incredibly naïve. I got so carried away with my lists and target dates that I backed myself into a corner. I was thinking, *"Hey, we can build Leg Up Farm and be open in 2004."* While thinking positive is a good thing, I went too far. I even printed that date in our brochure. On the cover. Oh well, as long as you learn from your mistakes, you won't make them again.

It didn't matter that we had to adjust our timeline for Leg Up Farm a bunch of times, because at least we were moving ahead. What mattered was *why* we were doing this. All I had to do was look at Laurie, driving to five appointments a week, dragging Olivia, Toby and Lauren along, and at Brooke, trying so hard to speak and walk, and I would remember that it would all soon be worth it for us and for thousands of other families like ours.

Sam and his reading buddies, 2012.

Live the Dream

A special section dedicated to all of the children that inspire me every day.

"Not many people can say that they look forward to going to work, or that they love their job, but I can! I love all of the children who come through our doors."

Michelle LaRose, Leg Up Farm Staff Member

Nathan & Sam at Leg Up Farm.

Sam's Buddy

Nathan, an eight-year-old boy with light brown hair lays his head on Sampson ("Sam"), a four-footed Leg Up employee. Sam is a retriever (technically he is a Labrador Retriever). His specialty is reading…that is, being read to. Sam and his owner, Kelly Maddox, work with kids like Nathan as part of our instructional reading program in Matthew's Town. You can usually find them lying next to the huge yellow dog house.

There, Nathan reads the children's book *Flat Stanley* (by Jeff Brown) aloud. Nathan pauses when he comes across a word he does not know, sounding it out slowly. Sam listens patiently and wags his tail encouragingly. Nathan drapes his whole body over Sam and reads the next page.

Since he started with Sam, Nathan has advanced two reading levels. Nathan's happy. His mom is happy. We're pretty sure Sam is happy too.

Trot!

"Don't let what you cannot do interfere with what you can do."

John Wooden

A week after Leg Up Farm opened, I met a five-year-old boy named Noah at an autism fair. He was with his mother, Lynne, and "Mammaw Maggie." Noah's Mammaw is a retired Marine, so she had instilled that fighting spirit in her daughter, Lynne, who uses it every day to help Noah with the challenges related to his autism.

Maggie told me about Lynne's great commitment to her son. "Lynne struggles financially, but, God love her, she will spend the very last penny if it means the possibility of hope for Noah to improve."

The day of the autism fair, Noah was in a special stroller, like the one I had for my daughter Brooke. I greeted them, and then I told Noah and his family about how this place, Leg Up Farm, was going to help them. We would support Noah by combining multiple therapies under one roof in the most amazing, child-friendly environment. I told them how our staff would work together to support their entire family, and that our outcomes would be better and happen faster. I told his family I had seen this dream clearly for the last 13 years.

Maggie remembered that day and how I spoke to Noah for the very first time, talking to him as few others had, as if he understood what I was saying. You see, Noah, like my Brooke, was unable to respond verbally. Like Brooke's jaw, Noah's looked as if it were frozen, and his body did not allow him to communicate by talking. However, because Brooke had taught me so much, I figured that Noah knew exactly what was going on even if it didn't look like he understood. I told him about Leg Up Farm's donkeys, miniature horses, and ponies. I trusted that he heard me.

When Noah was a baby, Maggie and Lynne almost lost him. Although he survived, the doctors gave them no hope for improvement. At his check-up, right before coming to Leg Up Farm, the developmental pediatrician said Noah would be at an 18- to 24-month level for the rest of his life and would never talk or reach any other milestones.

I am happy to say that doctor was wrong.

When Noah first started coming to Leg Up Farm, he came through the front door in his stroller. He was quiet, reserved, and did not speak; he appeared to be very fragile. However, like many children who come to Leg Up Farm, Noah started therapy and began to blossom.

Recently Maggie and I sat and talked about Noah. She was fighting back tears as she looked toward our riding arena and remembered a joyful moment. This particular moment was the day when Megan, our equine director, asked Noah, "Do you want to trot?"

And Noah replied, "Trot."

This is remarkable for two reasons. Noah had never said the word "trot" before, but more importantly, he had never answered *any* question verbally.

The great thing about the changes we witness at Leg Up Farm is that the kids keep getting better, and Noah's story is no exception. When Maggie and Lynne talk about how Noah has changed since he started coming to Leg Up Farm two years ago, they have a lot to talk about.

Maggie describes it "as if the sleepy part of his brain has come to life."

Noah is now seven years old, has a vocabulary of 50 words, and has mastered the art of putting two words together by saying things like "right here" and "thank you." Maggie calls Noah's therapists, Ms. Amy, Ms. Danielle, Ms. Megan and Ms. Amanda, his angels.

Maggie says, "Noah is walking better, his muscle tone is better, his speech is better, and he is even putting on his own shoes with his physical therapist, Ms. Amy." Though these may seem like small signs of progress, for Noah's family they represent a quality of life they hadn't dared hope for, and one that they are celebrating.

Perhaps the most beautiful word Lynne has ever heard is the word "Mom." Many parents take this for granted — but imagine how sweet that sound is to a mother who hears it, years later than usual, for the first time.

I can only imagine how she feels. I'm still waiting for Brooke to say "Daddy," but I know one day it's going to happen!

The Conductor

The iconic sound of the Addams Family theme music fills the classroom. It's Halloween, and Mr. Jeff is at it again. Known as the jazz go-to guy in our town, Jeff Stabley comes to Leg Up Farm every week to work his magic with the kids.

The children sit in a semi-circle and wait for the first note from his keyboard. They each have a role to play in the music, so they're eager.

"Okay, you," says Mr. Jeff to a little girl, "Hold your hand up. I want you to conduct the song. Are you ready?"

She nods in delight. "Now," instructs Mr. Jeff, "when you open your hand, the music will start. When you close it, it stops. Got it?" She nods again.

She opens her hand. Instantly the unmistakable *ba-da-da-dum* of the Addams Family theme starts. Everyone giggles. She closes her hand. Silence. She shrieks with delight.

"Me!" yells a little boy.

"Okay!" says Mr. Jeff. "GO!"

And the music starts and stops on his cue.

He calls on an older girl next. "Can you raise your arms? Good. Now, when you lower your arms, there'll be a big HUGE cymbal crash."

She makes everyone wait, breathless. She's in control of the music. Finally, when the room is tense with expectancy, she drops her arms to her lap. Smash! The cymbal sounds. She blushes and curves her arms over her head, hiding part of her face.

What's amazing about this is that the children in this classroom have limited mobility and function. There is very little they can do for themselves, so making something happen is a fairly novel feeling—and extremely empowering.

Mr. Jeff adapts everything for the group in front of him: "If you can't snap your fingers, stomp your feet. If you can't stomp your feet, move your head. If you can't move your head, blink." Everyone makes the music happen. They're learning something too, only that doesn't seem to be the point. The fun is the point. Isn't it?

*Tony Stewart with Cory & Allie Yahnke, 2005.
Photo by Penny Yahnke*

A NASCAR Fairy Tale

Brooke knew Allie Yahnke from the multi-disability support class they attended together in elementary school. Allie's parents had heard about the plans for Leg Up Farm and hoped that, one day, Allie would be able to go there with Brooke. They wanted to help.

In an unexpected twist, Allie's grandmother turned out to be a fairy godmother of sorts. Mary Yahnke was the former director of tourism for Inlet, New York, which may not sound like a natural fit for helping with Leg Up Farm since she lived hundreds of miles away. Yet when Allie was ten, Mary decided to write a letter to the managers of one of her town's yearly events. It was Zippy's Crusade for Kids, a charity started by the pit crew of NASCAR great Tony Stewart.

A few weeks later Mary received an invitation in the mail—along with some fabulous news. Zippy's had decided to donate money from their next fundraiser, the Snowmobile Charity Ride, to Leg Up Farm. The whole Yahnkes family attended and was presented with a $5,000 check. That week, Allie's picture appeared in the paper with the famous driver.

Nine months later, we recognized the Yahnkes publicly at our golf tournament. With every boost like this, we were one step closer to the Farm being built and actually opening.

Allie's story didn't end there. In late August 2012, I watched as she arrived at Leg Up Farm to start her first day of school in our secondary students life skills class.

Seven years after Allie and her family believed in the dream, she was *living* the dream. I spoke to the class, telling them the story, and reminding Allie of the part she had played in helping our center be built. She smiled and clapped. The look on her face told me she was proud of having been able to help. I was proud of her, too, and inspired to forge ahead.

My Horse

Drew came in as a five-year-old when we first opened. Although his father is a policeman, Drew loved firemen. He always wore a t-shirt with a bright red fire truck on it. Drew had dyspraxia, which affected his motor skills and coordination, among other conditions that had yet to be diagnosed.

At first, Drew was unsure of his surroundings and was intimidated by the horses and even our barn cats. We used to have to close the cats in the tack room so he could have his lesson. Drew finally got the courage to get up on a horse after his brother got on first. And then his transformation began.

When I first met Drew, I would try to say hi, but he would hide behind his dad's legs. The head of our therapeutic riding program, Megan, told me he could say about three words: "Mom," "Dad," and "No." As far as I could tell, "No" was his favorite word. He'd never made eye contact with any of us.

From time to time, I would drop in on lessons, and I noticed Drew was starting to give his horse commands. Another thing I noticed was that his eyes were now locked on Megan. One day I heard him put three words together and address them to her: "I am funny." Megan was thrilled. For a silent child to learn to respond to questions is progress. For him to initiate a conversation with eye contact—that was amazing.

Drew got so good on Xander, the horse he had begun riding, that they had to put him on another horse. However, Xander remained a favorite with Drew.

We have a rule in the barn: no running. When he first came, Drew had to be pushed around in a stroller because he was not able to walk well. We didn't expect that rule to be a problem with him. As he advanced, Drew began to walk more. The next thing we knew, he was running. He would zip down the barn aisle, looking for Xander's stall. He would stop, point, look at Megan, and say, "My horse is Xander." She would just smile; she didn't have the heart to tell him not to run, and neither did I.

I had another encounter with Drew that I'll never forget. Megan discovered that Drew loved fire trucks, so she asked the fire department down the street for a favor. In the middle of Drew's lesson, three firemen walked right into the arena in full gear. Drew could see their big yellow fire truck outside. He was so excited after his lesson, he forgot about being quiet. Walking over to him then, I said, "Hi, Drew!" Without hesitating he turned, looked at me, smiled, waved, and said, "Hi, Louie!"

Big Show

Reiley is five years old, and he has been coming to Leg Up Farm for a year. He has apraxia and sensory processing disorder, which basically means he takes in and interprets what he sees and hears differently, then has difficulty responding in appropriate ways.

For his part, Reiley is all about wrestling. Chances are, if you saw him, he'd be moving and whacking his wrestling figures against each other and spouting facts about his favorite guy, Big Show. Reiley's eyes got big when one of the staff told him he'd actually met Big Show. He agreed that he'd feel small, too, next to the seven-foot-tall wrestler.

Reiley's mom, Laurie, told me that before they starting coming to the Farm, "Reiley was really struggling. He wasn't getting what he needed from the therapists we took him to." He disliked going to a typical medical facility, and ended up being bounced around between providers a few times when therapists left. Because Reiley has what his mom calls "meltdowns," they've had trouble finding therapists who can communicate well with him. At Leg Up Farm, she says, "they're very tolerant when he does have these meltdowns.

You could put him with anybody here and he'd be happy."

Laurie explains that it's very different from the institutional hospital settings they used to travel to for therapy. Reiley exclaims, "It's like coming to a farm to play." They take him outside to the playground or to the fish pond, he can play with the barn cat, or he can watch the other kids ride horses.

Reiley has learned some new skills here: he can cut up his own hot dog now and cut a circle out with scissors. He's working on two other tasks: he can almost tie his shoes and zip up his jacket by himself. "The fact that he can do all this stuff," says Laurie, "is awesome."

It has also helped Laurie, who observed, "Reiley and I are treated like we are members of the family. Everyone greets everyone's kids when you come in. Plus they're always ready to help if I have a question about insurance, or if I need to cancel. They say, 'No problem!' Right from the start it was very easy, and everyone was so nice. They strategize with you, and they email you. It's not like: *Your hour is over, goodbye.*"

When Laurie's parents flew in for a visit from Scotland, they were very surprised when they arrived at Leg Up Farm. Laurie wasn't sure what they had expected, but she says they're now fans, and they're even wearing their Leg Up Farm t-shirts back in Scotland.

Cowboy Up

Walt has always been a cowboy at heart. Somewhere along the way — having sold his horses decades ago — he forgot who he was. So he perked up when his wife, Arlene, told him about Leg Up Farm and our need for help in the barn. "I was in a real funk at the time," Walt, who is retired, told me. "I was in a lot of physical pain, and I felt like my life had no purpose."

With no experience working with children with disabilities, Walt worried that he wouldn't feel comfortable. But he found he loved helping as he led the horses around the ring during lessons. He learned all the children's names, and they learned his.

For the past decade, Walt had been (in his words) "physically a wreck," suffering from severe chronic pain and unable to get around well. When he started volunteering, there were days when just keeping up with the horses hurt so much he had to stop. But because he felt like he was making a difference, Walt didn't give up. Because he wanted to keep working with the horses and the kids, he went back to his doctor, and discovered the pain was due to problems with the veins in his legs. He agreed to the surgery that was recommended, mainly so he could get back to the Farm. "I knew I had to do something to stay there."

"I've got to do this," he said to himself. "I've got to get back to Leg Up Farm." A month later, Walt returned to the barn. He was curious to see how one child he'd been working with was doing. He wondered if Katie would remember him.

Katie, waiting for her lesson, was petting Cheetah, one of the barn cats. Seeing Walt making his way down the barn aisle, Katie headed toward him. He saw her and stooped down, holding one hand up for their typical high-five greeting. Instead, Katie launched herself into his arms for a hug. The look on Walt's face—sheer wonder—revealed the soft heart hidden beneath his tough cowboy persona.

Walt headed over to check on another child who was having her lesson. Hannah had not been vocal when Walt had last been at the barn. Watching her ride, Walt noticed the instructor holding up colored circles labeled with riding commands. A red sign had the word "Whoa" printed on it. "Whoa!" said Hannah, and her horse stopped. Walt was floored. So much had happened in just a few weeks.

"When I saw that," he says, shaking his head, "it gave me chills. To see the progress they made with her was something else. I can't tell you how it's brought me to a different thought process. Just being near them brings me joy."

Now that he's back, Walt says his involvement has done a lot for him at home, too. "I'm not as abrasive as I was. I was angry, because of the pain. I'm fine now; I get up and look forward to being with the kids. Seeing their joy brings me joy, and being with the horses brings me joy."

Arlene agrees: "He's happy again. He has a passion again. He's great with the kids. He found something that really excites him, and it's helped him physically, emotionally, and psychologically. It's all just fallen together," she says. "He's a changed man."

Once again in his element, Walt just grins.

Come and Play

"Can you come over to play at my house?" This was a typical question for a child in many settings, but Anthony isn't your typical child. Anthony had been diagnosed with ADHD and Asperger's Syndrome, an autism spectrum disorder.

A year ago, Anthony had been a quiet ten-year-old, wrapped up in his own world. Today, his mother, Marcy, tells a different story: "Anthony's much more willing to open up. He feels very comfortable at the Farm. He'll go up to another child and ask for his phone number so they can get together."

She's amazed at the difference in Anthony since he's been coming to Leg Up Farm. Not only is she encouraged, her family has noticed a change. "They know that he's improving, and in school they say that he's more communicative," says Marcy. "Even my neighbors see it, and they notice his friends coming over, too."

Our Teddy Bear

We love our volunteers—all 400 of them—and they're all special. But occasionally we get lucky, and someone like Mike Budesheim shows up. Mike's the kind of guy who not only believes in the dream, he thinks of ways to make it even bigger. We named Mike, who is like a big teddy bear, our first Volunteer of the Year.

Here is what it comes down to: Mike does whatever it takes.

Before finding us, Mike had never been around horses. He took to it pretty fast, though, logging 519 volunteer hours in the first year; most of them in the barn. He'd never been around kids with special needs, either. No problem. Pretty soon he was the most popular guy in the barn.

Mike caught the Leg Up Farm bug quickly, and he's always thinking about something new for the kids. "I just want to keep it going," he told me.

One day Mike brought in *Bob Bear*, a puppet he and his wife, Sue, now use to get the kids interacting. Bob got so popular he now has a Facebook page.

Another time, Mike decided music would help. He plugged in his CD player, popped in a few kid-friendly tunes, and soon everyone was warming up muscles, responding to instructions, and improving coordination. (The kids thought they were just having a good time dancing to "The Wheels on the Bus Go Round and Round".)

Mike brings everything he has to the Farm, like his experience as a fisherman. This came in really handy when we were planning the Koi pond. He shrugs off compliments, saying, "If I can just contribute to helping a child achieve a goal and be able to enjoy the same things that I take for granted, it's all worthwhile."

He and his wife Sue, who also volunteers at Leg Up Farm, marvel at the changes they have seen. Mike concludes, "They do miracles at the Farm in every area every day; you cannot leave without a smile on your face or a tear in your eye every time. Without question, it's the most rewarding thing I've ever done."

A Safe Haven

"You can let your hair down here." These words come from Nichole Shue. With two active boys—both with sensory processing disorder and ADD or ADHD—she's constantly on alert, keeping tabs on their whereabouts. Marc, eight years old, and Collin, seven, come to Leg Up Farm twice a week.

While the boys are here, Nichole is grateful she doesn't have to worry about where they are: "They can't get lost here. They're not going to let them go out the front door without a parent, so you don't have to be worried about them running out into traffic."

Nichole calls Leg Up Farm "a safe haven." She told me, "It's a community of children just like mine. Your kids might be acting up and out of control, but they can run free here because people understand. They're free to be themselves."

Something Nichole appreciates just as much, is talking to parents who understand what it's like to have children with special needs. As a single mom with Multiple Sclerosis, Nichole finds it especially helpful to have their encouraging input: "There are parents here who support me. Other mothers have already gone through a lot of these things, so you tag team with another mother. You can say, 'This is the problem I'm having. How did you deal with it?' A while back, we were considering one avenue of help, but they would tell me, 'Oh, that didn't help at all,' so you avoid that. You can really communicate with the other mothers to find out different ways you can help your child."

Help is, after all, what they came here for, and the help they're getting nets impressive results. Nichole remembered, "Before we started coming here, my oldest son (Marc) hated reading. Ms. Kelly actually helped him get interested." Now Marc reads to Sam, a Labrador Retriever in our instructional reading program.

"He'll tell me all about Sam," explains Nichole. "It used to be a chore to get him to go to the library to pick out something he wanted to read. Then we found a collection of books about a dog named Sam, and he's up to the third book in that series. Now, he goes without an argument."

According to Nichole, Marc has really come out of his shell. "He was very sad there for a while. He was hating school. He wasn't interested in life except for athletics, and he couldn't be motivated to do much. He was really struggling. "Now," says Nichole, "Marc is so much more confident. He works hard and is seeing the progress, and I've seen quite a difference at home." Collin is thriving, too. When Collin comes to the Farm, he rides a horse named Dot, which he loves. He also reads to Sam.

"They both enjoy Ms. Toni at the front desk," says Nichole, smiling. "I don't get any arguing about coming here, either."

Trusting Tori

A young man—let's call him Justin—was diagnosed with a mental health condition that made his life challenging. For most of his life Justin had worked hard to shut people out. It was easier to do, he believed, than to let them in. Letting people in was scary. Life had taught him this from a very young age. As Megan, our therapeutic riding instructor, learned Justin's history, she discovered he had been through quite a lot of trauma.

In her job at Leg Up Farm, Megan pairs horses and riders with care. She looks at what each child and each horse has been through and has a way of sensing what each needs to learn. After some thought, Megan chose Tori, a Dun Appaloosa, for Justin to ride. She believed that Tori, who had been moved around from place to place while never really fitting in, felt misunderstood. Megan was pretty sure Justin felt the same way.

She matched them up, and they worked together for six weeks. As she watched, she saw a young man who had shut out the world gradually connect deeply with this particular horse. After a few lessons, Justin started what he called his "Journal for Tori," a scrapbook he filled with pictures of the speckled horse—pretty unlikely for a husky teenage boy.

As Justin rode Tori, he picked up on the way Megan worked with the horse, and he saw the way the horse responded. He could see that Tori trusted Megan. Initially withdrawn and sullen, Justin slowly began to open up. It seemed as if he had decided that, if Tori thought it was safe to trust Megan, maybe he could, too. Justin began to show that trust by sharing his story with Megan. He hadn't talked about it before. He began by showing Megan other entries he'd put in the scrapbook, images and words that revealed what had happened to him in his childhood. Megan learned that Justin had been through more in his short life than most people ever did in a lifetime.

Justin was making progress, so it was with dismay that, just a few weeks later, he was told he would be moving out of the area. When he came for the last time, he knew he had to say goodbye to Tori but it was clear he didn't want to. He radiated anger and disappointment. They were in the riding arena, and the lesson, not surprisingly, wasn't going well. Megan felt she could practically see the wall Justin had put up between himself and the horse.

Halfway through the lesson, she stopped. Justin looked up quickly, then looked away. Megan waited for him to look back, but when he didn't, she spoke, wanting to help him learn to express his grief.

"Are you bummed that this is the last time? That things didn't play themselves out the way you wanted them to?" she asked.

Justin looked down, scuffing the toe of his boot in the sawdust: "Yeah."

Megan continued, "Are you shutting everyone out because of it?"

Justin nodded, admitting this was true. Still looking down, he mumbled, "That's the only way I know." He paused. "It's easier that way."

Megan walked around to face him. "You know what?" she asked gently. "Maybe your horse needs you to say goodbye to her right now."

With that, tears began to run down Justin's face. After a few minutes, he looked at Megan, then turned his gaze to Tori. He took a few hesitant steps closer to Tori, and straightened his shoulders. He reached out his hand slowly, then patted the blaze on Tori's nose. A minute went by.

"I have to leave now," he whispered to the waiting horse, resting his head against her long neck. Justin swallowed hard, fighting more tears, and spoke again, barely audible: "I won't be back."

Just as his life had been tough, Justin's last encounter at the Farm had been tough too. But for Megan, it held great promise. Although it had been painful for Justin to say goodbye to Tori, she felt Justin had to learn to actually say it and not just leave. He had to learn a new way of relating...and of leaving.

Despite years of instability and abuse, this teenager had chosen to trust Megan and Tori. He had broken with his past and shared his story. He'd taken important steps, choosing to relate to Megan and Tori instead of letting his anger control him. He hadn't walked away as he had in the past, coping by shutting everyone out.

Justin's time with Tori had given him a glimpse of another way to live—even if this time, it was just learning how to say goodbye.

Megan witnessed Justin's transformation with joy. She sensed that both he and Tori had experienced some kind of closure, and a new way of ending: a loving, shared goodbye.

Who You Gonna Call?

It was time to build our playground. It was an ambitious one, a huge fairy-tale kind of a playground with lots of colorful stations and no barriers. We were going to need an army to build this thing, but we knew who to call.

In fall 2011, our community showed up—in a big way. They donated more than 8,000 hours of their time to assemble our accessible playground. Our regular volunteers (about 400) came, along with hundreds of new volunteers—1,000 in total.

Day one of work on the Leg Up Farm playground.

It was a daunting task, made more difficult by the hurdles Mother Nature threw at us during that season. We went from eight inches of snow to twelve inches of mud, with low visibility from fog in between!

From dawn till dusk, people came, drinking the coffee and cocoa we supplied, pulling hats down over their ears until you couldn't tell who was who, and following the ever-complicated assembly instructions. People were losing their shoes in the deep mud. Still, we did it in seven days. It was an incredible show of support.

The completed Leg Up Farm playground.

Bubbles for Brooke

It was an unusually warm day in November and Brooke wanted to go outside. We were at Leg Up Farm. Brooke's physical therapist, Lin, had been trying to get Brooke to rotate her trunk for a couple of months now. She's very stiff and doesn't turn her body, so Lin had come up with some different approaches.

One of them involved a burbling fountain we'd just put in next to the Koi pond. It was a big boulder with three holes where water bubbled up out of the rock, and so far it was a big hit with the kids who came to the Farm.

I knew how much Brooke loved water, so I helped her over to the fountain. But I didn't stop there. I asked her if she wanted to touch the water. She nodded vigorously, and with the ease that comes from years of doing just this, I lifted her over and placed her on the ground next to the fountain, putting her legs out straight in front of her.

I held her left side close to the fountain and gave her a cue, a nudge, to get her to touch the water with her right hand. Without hesitating, Brooke angled her arm right across her body and stuck her hand in the water. "That's great!" I said. Her eyes were wide with wonder and delight.

I moved Brooke to the other side of the fountain and held her right side against me, closest to the boulder. This time I didn't even have to give the cue. She reached across her trunk with her left arm and stuck her hand in the fountain, this time with a huge grin.

When I tried to end the session, Brooke had her own ideas. I was in the middle of picking her up when she suddenly lunged toward the fountain, and ended up sitting right on the part that was bubbling up, immediately soaking her clothes. But the sound I heard—jubilant laughter—made me burst out laughing as well. I let her sit there for a minute, relishing her joy. I saw Lin, inside, looking out at us and shaking her head. Then she gave me a thumbs up.

Brooke had done something hard on her own. She hadn't been thinking about how difficult it was for her to reach over like that—she had done it effortlessly. The beauty of such moments fills my heart, especially as I remember the long road we took to get to this point.

"She's finally here," I tell myself.

"We really did it."

10
Focus on the Next Step

"Louis has accomplished something at Leg Up Farm through the power of his will to get something out of nothing and take it forward."

Bill Shipley, Business Owner & Supporter

One thing I found out early on is that I'm really nothing special. In most areas, I was flying by the seat of my pants, learning as I went. I didn't know anything about setting up medical providers or negotiating with insurance companies or running a therapeutic children's center. I didn't know anything about building this type of facility either, but here I was trying to coordinate all of that. People thought I was nuts.

In hindsight, I *was* a little nuts. But I did my best with the knowledge I had, and I received help from many angels along the way. Without them, I wouldn't have gotten very far, and without a lot of determination and hard work, the dream would have died.

Although I have now seen many successes in life, it's not as a result of my schooling. In fact, I only went to college for 40 minutes.

My folks had it all set: I was going to play football, study, and graduate. I went, but I only attended one class—and then I withdrew.

Understandably, my dad was upset. He had paid his own way through school and knew the value of what he had learned there. He recognized the opportunity that was in front of me—one that many high school grads desperately wanted but would never have.

Another factor was that Dad knew firsthand how hard it was to go to college once you had a family. He didn't want me to have to try to split my time between work and school and family by having them all happen at once. He had done that, and he had found it a hard road. He hoped for a better life for me, and he had worked and saved and sacrificed over the years so I could have this chance. Dad just wasn't ready to give up on the college dream for me, and he felt strongly that I was not making the right decision. He also told me later that he hadn't wanted me to have to fight my way into a career when a degree could help open the door. He wanted to see me reach my potential and be able to grab every possible opportunity in life.

I hated to disappoint him and Mom, but I just felt I wasn't well suited for college. I wanted to *do something*, not sit in a classroom and listen. The road I chose has been one requiring perseverance and hard work. In the years since then, I've had the best education possible—that of learning by making mistakes.

After I left my one and only college class, I decided I needed to work extra hard. I guess I wanted to prove I could succeed without going the college route. At any rate, I applied for anything I thought I could do.

I got a job working with at-risk kids in the city. I was officially there to help them with gym, but what I was really doing was making sure that no fights broke out. That was from 1-3 p.m.

Then I got another job. From 3-5 p.m., I'd head over to help a high school with their wrestling team practice. That left evenings open, so I went back to an ice cream place where I had worked when I was 15. They hired me for the last shift, so I'd close up shop about 10 p.m. and sleep for a few hours. Extremely early the next morning I'd head over to…you guessed it, my fourth job. This one was at the Fox 43 television station—from 4 a.m. to noon.

The job at the TV station was the one I really wanted. My dad had been in television, working behind the scenes as well as for a time as a game show host and news anchor, and I wanted to follow in his footsteps. I had been hired for an entry-level job at the local station, working on the technical side of the business, but I wasn't planning to stay at that level. My ambition was to move into the Sales Department, but I was only 19. I remember the staff laughing at me because I was too young to drink at the Christmas parties, yet they knew I wanted to have one of the "big boy" jobs.

I wasn't a natural in sales, because, as I learned at Fox 43, sales happened as a result of good listening skills, and I had grown up talking. But I was willing to learn. I worked my way up into the Traffic Department there, logging the commercials and programming. With a small raise and a shift to a daytime schedule, I was now able to shed one afternoon job, but I still had one more step to get to where I wanted to be.

I begged the General Manager to let me try selling. He didn't think I could do it, so I made a deal with him: if I got my work done at the station and used my spare time there, could I try to sell station advertising time? He agreed, mostly because he didn't think I would sell anything, but I was on a mission: I wanted that sales job!

Even I was surprised when my first presentation netted a deal with a new client for $20,000. No one was laughing now. Three months later they let me onto the sales team where I could finally make enough money to drop the other part-time jobs.

In between my first job at the TV station and my final promotion into sales, I filled a variety of roles there. As I observed what everyone did, I learned how important each person's role was, from the receptionist to the production manager, in providing great customer service. I developed a respect for each person, and saw each job as an important part of the whole.

When I was promoted to Account Executive, I had just turned 21 and was the youngest member of the sales force — by about a decade! In order to learn how to excel, I watched the other salespeople to see what their strengths were. One was great with the financial side of things. His contracts were always perfect. Another was really good at knowing how to satisfy her customers, and she got great comments from them. I learned what they did well and noted what could be done better. I decided to try to replicate the positive qualities of each person on the team so that I could become a better Account Executive.

A few years later, I made a move to the Fox 45 television station in Baltimore, which was an hour away. I loved what I did, and I was overjoyed when I was promoted to National Sales Manager there. From there I held a few different management positions including a job at Comcast Spotlight, another media company, overseeing four different sales offices. I learned a lot there, too, especially about planning and strategy — something that helped me in my upcoming role as President of Leg Up Farm.

I could never have foreseen where my career would take me, and I didn't have a framed diploma on my wall that proved I had learned "the right things". But I discovered that, because of my experience and the lessons I'd learned, I possessed everything I needed to succeed.

11
Ch-Ch-Ch Changes

> *"Normally my son is anxious and upset. But no matter how bad his day is, you have an entirely different child when he comes to Leg Up Farm. This is like home to us, this is where we come to relax. It helps us get through each day."*
>
> Loren Rutkowski, Parent

Once Brooke was diagnosed, there were a lot of changes in our family's life. I'm not talking about the kind of changes that mean you have to, say, go to a cheaper barber or put off buying a vacation home. I'm talking about the kind of changes that put you and your family high on the stress scale. I'm pretty sure we were off the chart.

Our time began to fill up with medical appointments. Actually, that's an understatement. Our schedule became so full that we could barely remember where we were supposed to be on a given day. Laurie had already resigned from her job to take care of the kids, and I resigned from mine to take a job closer to home.

Every week there were at least five separate places we had to go—just for Brooke's therapy and care. There was physical therapy. Occupational therapy. Speech therapy. There were monthly blood tests to verify the current diagnosis and to check other diagnoses. Specialists wanted to see us at multiple appointments to measure Brooke's legs so they could cast customized braces. We could see all of this wearing on Brooke. She was trying so hard—to walk, to speak, to grasp things with her hands, to feed herself. She could sense that the whole family had to take extra trips just for her, and she was grateful for everything we did for her. She kept trying to please us. But her body just wouldn't cooperate. And she would have moments when she would simply give up in frustration.

As care for Brooke became increasingly complicated and time-consuming, we adjusted to the "new normal". Vacations became rare—and really tricky. Would Brooke escape from our hotel room in the middle of the night? She was unable to speak, so she wouldn't have been able to ask for help to find her way back to the room.

To make sure this never happened, when we were out of town, we slept with our legs across Brooke's legs, so we would feel her move and wake up. We put bells on the door knob. We put a chair in front of the door. We put the mattress on the floor. We rearranged all of the furnishings, so anything dangerous would be out of harm's way.

Even back at our house, we had to take a second look. Was our home really safe? Would Brooke go out the front door and get lost? We put alarms on every door, so we would know if one of them opened. We put up a maze of gates in our house, creating safe areas for Brooke. But our other kids were just that—kids. What if they forgot to lock a gate, even once? What if they left the front door open, as children do? We found ourselves constantly reminding Toby, Olivia and Lauren to shut all of the gates and doors. Likewise, just as new parents baby-proof their environment, we had to make sure we didn't leave anything around that Brooke could put in her mouth.

Even up to age 16, she would still try to eat things she shouldn't eat. Leaving an empty bag of chips or even a water bottle cap around could result in Brooke choking. We were on constant alert.

Meanwhile, we were referred to a neurologist's office, where they ran MRI scans and conducted sleep studies. Our errand list grew: trips to the pharmacy, meetings with county case workers, sessions with therapeutic support staff to help us get through the day, plus the normal pediatric routine. The worst part was the ongoing stress of not understanding what the future would hold.

Our insurance didn't cover Brooke's nutritional needs. Her body needed all of the help it could get, so we loaded up on supplements and antioxidants to give her the extra boost she needed, and bought organic food to limit her exposure to toxins. Again, we didn't mind sacrificing for Brooke, but the extra expense squeezed our budget.

We spent a lot of time on the phone each month just getting authorizations for services. We were pushed into a confusing network of support where everyone seemed to function separately. I call it "navigating the web of confusion". At every level, whether the county, the state, or federal government, everyone meant well and wanted to help, but they had conflicting ways of getting there.

As we sat in the many waiting rooms, I would ask other parents, "If you could create the ultimate therapy center for children with special needs, what would you do?"

"I'd put everything in the same building so we wouldn't have to drive around," one mom told me. Another wished the services were all free, and another said she wanted to give all her insurance paperwork to someone who would handle everything for her. A young father of a boy with autism said he wanted a place where his son would be accepted and where his daughter would have something fun to do. A single mom wished for the opportunity to talk to other parents, while the parents of one girl said they would love to have some kind of creative therapy for her, like music or dance.

They all had ideas and so did I. We talked about what it could be like, and the dream grew.

Our first official logo.

12

Do the Right Things Every Day

"Great works are performed not by strength, but by perseverance."

Samuel Johnson

My father and I were sitting in my kitchen having some pumpkin pie after Thanksgiving dinner. Every year he and I inevitably ended up in the kitchen together, after the turkey was put away, and we'd talk about what was going on in our lives. This year, our conversation took a different turn.

I was telling him about my dream for Leg Up Farm. His response was, "Are you crazy? You have a good job and you have to support your family. Why would you risk everything?"

My parents have not walked the easiest path in their lives. There were many challenges right from the start. They have made it work — for 42 years so far — but at the beginning, well, it was a struggle.

My dad's life changed forever when he first heard my mom sing during practice for their high school musical. It was 1969. Apollo 11 had just landed on the moon, and Elvis was making a comeback, but what captivated my father was Mom's singing voice. It was a thing of beauty, and so was she. Dad was two years ahead of her and was involved in the musical, too. More of an actor than a singer, he was happy just to be on stage—especially if it meant being near Mom.

One night during rehearsal, my dad was backstage. He walked over to a chair right next to where my mom was going over her lines. Then he waited to catch her eye, and called her over. He asked her if she'd like to go out sometime. She answered by sitting in his lap (she thought he was really cute).

My dad was hoping for a job in show business, so he would practice his impersonations on my mom. One time he imitated Neil Armstrong walking on the moon, making the sounds of his boots and transmissions from mission control. She was his best audience, laughing until tears rolled down her cheeks.

Their romance flourished, and all too soon, in 1970, they were married, and had a baby—me. Mom was still in high school when she got pregnant.

My father didn't give up his dream of being in broadcasting, so after Mom had me, he packed all of us up and took us with him to Penn State. Studying and working full-time to support us while putting himself through school didn't leave him much time to enjoy his new family, but he and Mom made the best of it.

For "entertainment," Dad recalls walking around Nittany Mall, dreaming of the days when they would be able to buy something.

They would splurge on a treat — one pretzel for 30 cents for the three of us to share. Mom found simple things for us to do, taking me hiking or feeding the ducks at the nearby lake.

My father worked any job that he could find to pay for schooling, which he did without taking out any loans or getting any financial aid. He began as a freshman working at Mr. Donut starting at three a.m., then heading to class at eight. For a couple of years he was a DJ at a few radio stations in the area, proudly adopting the moniker, "the Mouth of Center County." On weekends he spun records anywhere he could to make extra money — at bars, parties, and high school dances.

My mom's choices for work were limited because she was at home taking care of me, and we had only one car. Ever willing to do her part, she took in ironing, making four dollars for each basketful of clothes she painstakingly pressed. To stay within our budget, we ate a lot of navy beans in those days. At just 20 cents a bag they were a bargain, so we had baked beans, boiled beans, bean soup, chili with beans, and anything else you could possibly make with beans.

I was a curious kid, experimenting with anything I found lying around our apartment. *Would my socks go down the toilet?* I wondered. *Yes,* I realized, *they would.* (My parents did not appreciate the clogged pipes — or the plumbing bill.) One time I plugged what I thought was the record player into an outlet. It turned out to be the cord for the cuckoo clock. That did not go well, as the clock caught on fire. Cuckoo clocks weren't cheap, and neither were plumbers, so I guess I was the exact opposite of a help when it came to our budget.

*Louie, Mom & Dad,
Penn State Graduation, 1974.*

After Dad graduated, we moved back to our hometown. He looked for a new job, and it seemed impossible for them to catch up with all the bills. He continued to DJ on the weekends at weddings and special events. When I got older, he would bring me along to help carry stuff—speakers, turntables and many boxes full of records. (In those days it wasn't possible to have 4,000 songs loaded onto an iPod that fit in your hand, so there was a lot of heavy equipment to lug around.) He paid me a few dollars when I helped, but really, it was just a good excuse for us to spend time together.

Dad came to my football practices and games as well, and he even coached our team for a few years when I was little. We would talk football, and he would teach me what I had done well and what I needed to do better. We always ended these practices with a cherry snow cone.

"Dad was always by my side," (Louie is #12).

Mom stayed at home, dedicating all of her time to me and my two sisters Erin and Carrie. She ran me from one sports practice to another and drove my sisters to Pony Club as well as to a never-ending succession of horse shows. I find this is something you don't really appreciate until you are doing it for your own children. I see now that Mom was incredible!

All of this hard work set a great example for me. I was able to see how they both sacrificed for one another and for us kids and upheld strong family values. Both of them were also very caring toward others in need, encouraging me and my sisters to volunteer from a young age. I remember being so proud of my whole family in 1988, when I entered the Athletes vs. MS event. We all worked to raise money for this cause, and we set a new record. I never forgot the good feeling that helping others brought.

As I look back, the sacrifices my parents made, and the values they hold dear have shaped me and prepared me for my life's work with Brooke and all of the children who come to Leg Up Farm. My parents have also contributed their time, their energy and their encouragement to this dream. They are truly angels.

"Mom, still my biggest supporter."

13

A Bureaucratic Angel

"Leg Up Farm is – and always will be – the biggest success story that I will ever see in my career."

Nancy Englehart

Late one afternoon a woman ran down the hall of the state office building where I was waiting, grabbed me and shuffled me quickly into the office of the deputy secretary for the Pennsylvania Department of Economic Development.

"You have fifteen minutes to talk," she whispered urgently, "and you need to speak from your heart."

The woman was Nancy Englehart, who worked in an old state office building, and I still don't know how she got me into that office. It was nearly impossible for someone like me to get a meeting with someone that high up in the Pennsylvania State Government. Yet Nancy made it happen in one day.

Because of that meeting, in the final funding round of the fiscal year, we received approval for a grant in the amount of $60,000. I felt like whooping with joy!

I had gotten in to see Nancy by relentlessly begging. My luck was that she was the one who answered the phone when I first called. I could practically hear her groan as I, just one of the hundreds of callers with wacky ideas wanting money, announced that this would be the first grant I had ever applied for, and that I would be writing it myself. But she listened with her heart and patiently answered my questions…all of them.

I questioned everything, because this was how I learned. I would finish talking to her and hang up the phone, look at the application again, write down more questions, and call her right back. I was unwilling to take a chance on mailing it, so I hand-delivered the application to Nancy myself. Honestly, sometimes the simplest acts can change the course of your life. Delivering the application by hand was one of these.

Nancy's desk was located in a cavernous hallway—I could hear my footsteps echoing as I walked toward this woman who would become a touchstone in my long journey. As we talked in person, she was very patient as I explained again about Brooke and what I wanted to do.

I learned a critical lesson from Nancy. If I gathered people around me who would collaborate on the dream, and if I followed up every lead, I would gain her respect and eventually we would make something happen.

I did whatever she suggested. If she had told me to stand on top of the giant gold dome of the state building to get someone's attention, I would have gotten a crane and done it. Fortunately she was more reasonable than that, forever giving me names of people I should call. I called every single one. And when she recommended that I get the support of my State Senator and Representative to help go for a particular grant, I went for it. I got other people on board, and the dream was no longer just one man's crazy idea.

We were refused for the grant I applied for — twice. But there was one more opportunity for a yes. I collected more letters, this time from our State Representatives, County Commissioners, State Senators, and one of our U.S. Congressmen.

By then it was May of 2000. I decided to visit Nancy again — she had to know a way to make this happen. I pleaded my case one last time, and she listened compassionately. That's when she told me to wait and she would get me in to see her big boss. She said she didn't know how long it would take but promised she would let me have a chance to tell him my story. So I sat in an ancient chair and then paced that corridor for hours.

That's when Nancy came and grabbed me. She guided me through that door, and I met with her boss. For fifteen minutes, he listened. I told him about the kids, about the great need, and about the dream. I left feeling as if he had heard me, but it would be another month before I would know whether our conversation had changed anything.

A month later, I had just arrived at work and was getting my morning coffee in the break room. As I usually do, I glanced at the local paper, skimming it for items of interest. The words I saw in the Local section made my heart pound: "Leg Up Farm has received a $60,000 grant." I felt like jumping up and down, but I just grabbed my cell phone to call Laurie, and we celebrated together for a minute, laughing through our tears.

Throughout the grueling, 13-year journey of working to open Leg Up Farm, I popped in and out of Nancy's office again and again. She was another angel who never gave up on me, and she believed in our dream when few others did.

To this day she sends me upbeat emails, giving me that little lift that can make the difference between a day heading toward frustration and a day filled with possibilities.

Nancy & our therapy horse, Scooter.

Do You Own Land in York County?

"Giving Children a Leg Up on Life"

- Would you like to preserve your land?
- Would you like to help children & families with special needs in our community?
- York County will be a better place to live because of you!

Leg Up Farm is looking for 50+ acres for a non-profit therapy & rehabilitation center for children with special needs. The unique farm environment will be a key component to our plan.

For additional information, call
843-8341 or e-mail ljcastriota@legupfarm.org

14
Land Free for the Asking

"Leg Up Farm will be a dream come true, not just for the people who have made the building come about, but for all of the families whose dreams are just beginning. These children are going to come to believe in themselves so that they can achieve and develop the talents that they have. And they will only be able to do that with the resources that they get from Leg Up Farm."

        Dr. Allen R. Miller
        Director, WellSpan Behavioral Health

We needed a place families dealing with special needs could call home. In 2000 and 2001, I looked at literally hundreds of properties to find the perfect home for Leg Up Farm. I'd drive by every farm and slow down. If you were behind me, I was the "idiot" going five miles an hour.

I kept a list of my top 20 possibilities, but I must have chased down more than a hundred dead ends. I knocked on strangers' doors and sent letters to people I had never met, asking them to donate their land to an unknown start-up charity.

I told them how hundreds of children who needed a leg up would thrive at the place we would build. Some of the land owners responded with faith in the dream as I explained that we would have children riding gentle horses, working on coordination on balance beams, and role-playing with puppets.

They were drawn in as I explained why we needed a place where these kids' whole families could come and have fun together while they waited for one of their children to learn how to walk on our hiking trails or work on reading skills.

I toured properties, like an actual purchaser, with real estate agents who looked at me like I was a little crazy. At one point I threw an ad in the paper, sending an outright plea into what felt like just empty space. Sure enough…nothing. I already had a vision of what I wanted the property to look like, but I couldn't find it. Still, I wasn't willing to settle.

We needed the perfect property. Everything had to be just right: Not too close to the city. Not too far away. Accessible, available…and oh, did I mention this? Really, really cheap.

We established a "Goldilocks Principle" — we were looking for something "just right". That meant, for Leg Up Farm, the terrain couldn't be uneven, and this being Pennsylvania, some of the properties we visited had some serious hills! In order for our kids to be able to get around the property, it would have to be as flat as a pancake.

We knew we wanted the Farm out in the country where kids could enjoy the healing power of nature. At the same time, it had to be near the highway. Some land we looked at was so far out there I got lost trying to find it, and I'm pretty good at directions. No way our clients would find it.

One tempting plot of land had no driveway—and no way to put one in. Another was located right along the interstate. Easy to locate, sure. But so expensive we'd never be able to afford it.

Brownstone sites (former industrial sites) could be had for a song. As in, $1. But we'd have to pay millions for clean-up, and we'd likely uncover some strong chemicals—substances that would irritate our kids, many of whom had cranked-up sensory issues and allergies. Another dead end.

I kept driving around, looking. Sometimes I would bring Brooke along. She loved riding in the car, because she liked the vibrations she felt as we swooped over hills that made her stomach fly and bounced over potholes that made the whole vehicle shudder.

Looking back, 18 months wasn't a long time to find land. But what made it hard was not knowing whether anything would pan out. So we were always wondering, *Are we going to find anything anywhere? Are we being too picky? This could take five more years. Do we have the determination to get through the next five years if we don't find something?* The whole endeavor started to feel like we were fishing in a stream that might not have any fish in it. Most days we could throw out the line and think, *Yes! We will find something.* Other days it was like all our hook caught was an old tire.

One day in the Fall of 2000, the phone rang. I picked it up and heard a woman's voice: "I have some property," she said. "I don't know if you'll like it, but would you like to come and see it?"

The woman's name was Barb Warren. The day I drove up and saw the land, I had to laugh at the way she had presented it. *Like it?* Goodness, what was *not* to like?

Barb had heard about Leg Up Farm at a meeting where we'd been investigating another site that hadn't worked out. When Barb read in the paper that we hadn't gotten the land, she picked up the phone and dialed my number.

It was convenient—close to the major highway—but secluded. Located in Mt. Wolf, a small town just north of York, it was gorgeous, with beautiful views of rolling hills, but flat enough for our kids and close by enough for our parents. Barb and I walked around her farm, and she mentioned donating maybe ten acres and letting us use the rest of the property for activities. I couldn't decide whether to hug her or cry. I cried.

There were many hurdles in the following months, but fortunately, Barb was not only an angel, she was a saint. Every month I'd bring her yet another document to sign. There were documents to subdivide the property, applications for a special zoning exception, papers discussing run-off, and details about how to incorporate a turning lane into the site. If you've been through this process, it's horrible. The bureaucracy was not working with us, and at times it was so bad that it became local news.

The *York Sunday News* ran an editorial criticizing the township for its attitude and lack of cooperation. "Really?" it seemed to be saying, "You're not helping the kids because of what? A turning lane?" People on both sides of the issue were getting seriously cranky.

It would have been easy for Barb to say she was done with being in the public eye. But she never did. She stuck with us for — get ready — nine more years until we finally opened. Barb ultimately gave us 18 acres, because, as our plans evolved, she could see that the kids would need a lot more space. Plus she gave us permission to use even more of her land for whatever we needed. Today, thanks to Barb, we have the most amazing home for Leg Up Farm. Not only that, but to this day Barb gets up every morning at six a.m. to feed our horses — seven days a week! If you're going to build a horse farm and you're lucky enough to have an angel's help, it's a plus if the angel also loves horses.

15
Step by Step

"One hundred years from now it will not matter what kind of car I drove, what kind of house I lived in, how much I had in my bank account, or what my clothes looked like. But one hundred years from now the world may be a little better because I was important in the life of a child."

Forest Whitcraft

Mildred Overbaugh wasn't the corporate type. She was more the grandmotherly type. Small, in her 80s, and smiley. Not your typical go-to person for getting a huge project going. But Mildred had a grandson named Dan, and because of him she bought the dream quicker than an auctioneer proclaims, "Sold!"

Dan was no longer the little boy Mildred remembered coming to her house on Sundays for dinner. Back then, every time he came, he would head straight outside, and Mildred would follow. There was a stream nearby, and it was there that the boy who didn't seem to fit in anywhere else found his refuge. Dan would sit on a rock with his grandmother listening to the burble of the water until it was time for dinner. Then Mildred would take his hand and they would walk back to the white farmhouse together.

Mildred's property was sprawling and hilly, and her house had a big front porch where she liked to sit and look out over the farm. Mildred understood the healing power of nature and regretted that there was no place like Leg Up Farm for Dan, who now lived in a group home and spent much of his time indoors.

She wanted to make Leg Up Farm happen for all the other "Dans" who were still children, kids who would grow and learn and surpass everyone's expectations, even their own.

Right after she read about the dream in the newspaper, she began writing me letters of encouragement. I had no idea who she was, but boy was I glad she had picked up that newspaper!

Mildred was a reader. She would clip articles from the paper she thought might interest me and send them to me. When it came time for our silent auctions, Mildred looked around her home until she found something that would really help us out: a beautiful antique trunk that had been in her family for generations. What a gift.

One of the coolest things, though, was that Mildred wrote many letters to businesses to try to get the Farm going. I remember landing a big donation many years ago just because Mildred took the time to write to a business owner.

When we finally opened, I dropped by to tell Mildred what it was like. She sat me down with a big bowl of beef stew and listened with a shared pride in what we'd made happen as I described the kids and the horses and the building. A few weeks later, she brought Dan so they could see it for themselves, and they spent some time hanging out on our porch.

Dan is now in his late 20s, and unfortunately Leg Up Farm doesn't offer services for adults — yet. When we can, Dan will be my first call.

Mildred & Dan at Leg Up Farm in 2011.

16
A Spirit of Giving

*"I wanted to turn the Potter family's
tragedy into a positive."*

Jack Lehr, Co-Founder of the
Matthew Allen Potter Memorial Golf Tournament

The night before September 11, 2001, the Potters, a family from York, Pennsylvania, set out for the York Fair with their neighbors, Jack and Kim Lehr (and the Lehr's three-year-old son Jack III). The Potter children, Matthew (age seven), Ryan (age six), and Natalie (age five) had grown pumpkins and entered them in the agricultural pumpkin contest, so everyone was very excited, in anticipation of what prizes their pumpkins might have won.

After viewing their pumpkins and award ribbons, it was off to see the farm animals and then get some dinner. As the children rounded the corner, trying to decide what to eat, they saw a roller coaster with a "car-racing" theme. Matthew was a huge fan of NASCAR, so he was drawn to the black-and-white checkered theme of the ride. Although they had not planned on riding any of the rides that afternoon, Matthew, Ryan, and Natalie ran to the entrance and boarded for a quick ride.

With growing alarm, the adults saw the ride suddenly speeding out of control. The next sequence of events occurred within seconds, but left a lasting, heart-breaking image in the minds and hearts of the Potter and Lehr families. Matthey, Ryan, and Natalie were involved in a terrible accident.

All three children were quickly taken to the first aid center of the York Fair, and Matthew was rushed to the Trauma Center of York Hospital, where he tragically passed away. With the help of the Lehr family and their pediatrician, and after tests were run at the hospital, Ryan and Natalie were released to their parents' care. Late that night, the incomplete Potter family left the hospital, and their lives had changed forever.

Still mourning for Matthew the following spring, Jack invited us to a picnic at his house. He said he had an idea for Leg Up Farm. Heart-sick and wanting to do something concrete, he proposed a golf tournament in Matthew's honor, with the proceeds to benefit the Farm.

All of this sounded good, especially since he said he'd organize it. But when he set the date for the one-year anniversary of the accident—just five months away—I balked.

Working in television, I'd run my share of events, and I told him that schedule was just plain nuts. I actually tried to talk him out of it. Jack was naïve, I thought, believing in that kind of timeline. Looking back, I see the irony—I'm the one with the crazy timeline people are usually trying to talk out of doing things!

It turns out, I had underestimated Jack. On September 19, 2002, the first annual Matthew Allen Potter Memorial Golf Tournament took place.

With a community golf event, you're lucky to raise $5,000. Jack blew me away with his results: over the next five years the tournament ran, it raised $160,000 for Leg Up Farm. I have no idea what we would have done without those funds; they kept us going.

At the first tournament, I got up and announced that Leg Up Farm was going to open soon. In fact, every year, for five years, I got up and said that. Jack kept helping, and the Potter family kept believing in the dream in their son's memory.

Today, because of an angel named Jack and the Potter family, hundreds of special kids benefit. They form relationships with their therapists and our volunteers that empower them, and they learn real-life skills in our interactive play center, which we named Matthew's Town. A tribute to the Potter's son, Matthew, this life-size pretend town helps kids gain confidence, strength, and abilities they can use to become more independent.

Ben simulating pumping gas in Matthew's Town, 2012

17
Work at the Dream

*"If you have built castles in the air, your work
need not be lost; that is where they should be.
Now put the foundations under them."*

Henry David Thoreau

When it came to raising funds, we did anything anyone could think of for the Farm. And I mean anything. Bake sales. Designer baskets, silent auctions. Employers matching service hours. Selling chocolate bunny tins. Tickets for snow tubing and car washes. Subs, pizzas. Giving pony rides. Making crafts. Our faith-based neighbors helped us out, too: a cookbook, an old fashioned hymn sing-along.

My own ideas were definitely iffier. I began playing the lottery, hoping for the Big Win. I'd run down to Rutter's and buy a Powerball and a Cash 5 ticket every single week, hoping for wads of cash. Walking out with the ticket, I'd envision how we would spend the winnings on building Leg Up Farm and how easy this would make things. But the Big Win never came!

We called everyone we knew—and many we didn't. We wrote to what felt like a *gazillion* people. Gradually some funds trickled in. It wasn't the lottery, but at least we could pay our light bill.

One day my research turned up a new possibility—a grant related to disabilities that would help launch our education-related therapies. I could practically see the sunlit rooms where our staff would help children use a speech device to say the words their lips couldn't form. I pictured our friend's son, reading to a therapy dog. I could see it!

I drove straight down to the Capitol building in Washington D.C. that day and walked right into my senator's office. Who needed an appointment? I was here for the kids.

So okay, I didn't get to see my senator, but I talked to someone who told me to talk to someone else who…well, you get the idea. I ended up walking around to a bunch of government buildings and telling the story of the dream to anyone who would listen.

I told them about Brooke and how it broke my heart that she spent most days cramped up in a car on her way somewhere that wasn't helping much. I explained how our facility would be different—how it would be engaging, family-friendly, and educational in a powerful way.

I went home that day, unsure whether anyone had truly understood the dream enough to help us take the next step. Fortunately, my trip to D.C. ultimately paid off—on January 22, 2004, we received a disability education grant for $175,000.

As we began to have success with Leg Up Farm, Brooke, who had been diagnosed when she was one, was now eight. Yet she was not really like an eight-year-old. I would look at her sweet face and feel a kind of panic, because it felt like we were losing valuable time — those early years can make such a difference in speech and mobility. If we couldn't get the Farm opened soon, we'd have to get working on adult programs, or she would have nowhere to go when she turned 21.

Then there were the medical bills for us and for others. The longer it took us, the longer some families would have to fork over expensive co-pays they couldn't afford…or deny their child much-needed therapy. The thought of those lost opportunities saddened us because we knew what it was like to have a child who wasn't getting the help she needed to thrive. We had friends who were going through the same thing, and we wanted something better for them, too.

In 2006, we hit a brick wall. We ran completely out of funds. Our employees no longer had a job. I went out to my car after laying off our only two employees and I just sat there, I didn't know what to do.

My full-time day job, the one that supported my family, had also gotten really stressful. The economy was crashing, and the last thing our clients wanted to buy was TV advertising — at that point, they were more worried about paying their own employees.

I took a new management job in Washington D.C. and was commuting two hours each way to work and coming home to bathe the kids and put them to bed while Laurie did her barn chores.

I wondered how long we could keep this up.

The dream was fading fast.

18
Never Stop Believing

*"Daddy never gave up; he wouldn't.
He said the community needed it
and he was going to do it."*

Olivia Castriota

"When are you going to think about shutting this down?" This question came about halfway through 2007, and it caught me off guard even more because it came from Dee, my friend and the first Leg Up Farm employee. Since she was off the payroll completely (at this point, there was no payroll), I had personally been doing everything from writing grants to paying bills to keep everything going.

I turned to our Board of Directors whose members had always exhibited faith in the dream. However, this many years into the process, because of the never-ending hurdles we kept encountering—many of the members began to doubt whether Leg Up Farm would ever be built. One board member resigned.

At the time, we felt things might end here. No Farm. No help for Brooke. I modeled a positive attitude, but at night the negative comments from our first fundraising study were circling in my head. I was restless, kicking the covers into tangles, keeping Laurie from a good night's sleep as well.

The words I heard over and over were the words of the best and most generous people in our town, who somehow failed to connect with the dream. How could they hear about Brooke and the other kids with challenges and not be moved?

I think the main problem was that we appeared to be fighting a losing battle. It wasn't that there weren't services at all for kids like Brooke. There were. And it wasn't that philanthropists didn't have the good of the children at heart. They definitely did. It was more that, after ten years and no end in sight, they weren't willing to invest in something that looked like it would never happen.

But I was fuming. I knew there were thousands of families in the area who needed our services. There were over 15,000 children in our county and the next one over who had been identified with special needs. There were another 30,000 or so kids, if you included Harrisburg to the north, and Lancaster to the east.

We conducted another study because we wanted to hear from the parents of these children. We found out that *half* of them wanted services but couldn't afford them because they didn't have insurance, or the services weren't covered. Many weren't getting services at all.

Their words were packed with *angst*, and they echoed with a sense that they'd been abandoned. Here are a few examples of what we heard.

- *Our son is non-verbal, and no one is able to help us.*

- *My child's recreational and social needs are just not being met, and I don't know what to do.*

- *I have never found a program that really meets my son's needs.*

- *No one wants to help children 13 and older.*

- *It would be helpful if you could have a place where you could go talk to a human being.*

- *You just have to put your foot down and advocate for your child because you can't get anyone to listen.*

One day, these parents' comments wouldn't stop rattling around in my head, so I did what I usually do: I went for a run. My typical route was 2-3 miles along the country roads near our home. It's pretty hilly there, and I had a challenging course I loved.

That day I set off a little faster than usual, my feet beating a rhythm to the words from the fundraising study. They just didn't get it! How could they not see the need? Man, was I mad. I passed the fence where I usually turned around but I just kept going. I still felt like punching something.

I ran all the way out to the main road before I turned around. I was breathing pretty hard. By the time I got home, I'd gone over 4 miles and it was pitch black, but my frustration and anger had ebbed.

My lungs ached and my legs were tired, but I felt the tension leaving my body. My mind, though, was another story. It was going a million miles a minute.

New possibilities flooded my brain, and after I got back home, I took out a pen and started writing. Maybe we could use the USDA loan program that I had learned about earlier in the year. We could use the study we'd done, the one where we'd talked to parents of kids with special needs. Maybe their voices could get through, along with the support of healthcare providers in the area who also said there was a need. These things would help us get loan approval.

Sometimes you need to shift your perspective to make it over hurdles in your path. We decided to build Leg Up Farm first and trust that the support would come. The dream would work—we knew it.

Much later, a reporter came by to interview us. She asked my daughter Olivia whether she thought I had ever been tempted to quit. Olivia said, "Daddy never gave up; he wouldn't. He said the community needed it and he was going to do it."

Even though things sometimes looked bleak, Olivia was right. I was determined.

19
The Last Puzzle Pieces

*"Great things are not done by impulse,
but by a series of small things brought together."*

Vincent van Gogh

We got our *big* break on November 13, 2008. USDA held a press conference announcing their approval of our $5 million loan. We could start building! Not bad for a new nonprofit like ours—with no assets to our name.

We could now envision the riding arena, a light-filled lobby, enthusiastic therapists, and even donkeys. My grandmother had decided what we needed at the Farm were miniature donkeys, and she had purchased two extremely cute foals: Dominic and Isaiah. She hand-fed them with bottles so they would get used to people and let kids pet them. Seeing her trying to slide Dominic up onto her lap for his feeding was one of the funniest sights I've ever seen.

On September 10, 2009—the magical day we actually took our shovels and started digging where children would soon play, we stood around and listened to speeches lovingly delivered by many people. But the one that touched me the most was by my youngest daughter Lauren, who had stayed up late the night before writing a speech she gave with the poise of a child much older than her 11 years.

> *Brooke, my sister and best friend, has been my inspiration by always persevering and keeping a smile on her face no matter what her struggles are. In our lives, we all have struggles, but no matter how hard it gets for you, plenty of other people have it worse. So the next time you have a bad day, focus your energy on helping someone else.*

Brooke was now 13 years old and helped me dig my shovel into the dirt, officially celebrating groundbreaking. What a feeling!

Groundbreaking, September 2009.

First we dug. Site work followed, then stone, then concrete and paving, then framing, windows and shingles. Things were getting really fun. Grand opening in 2010: here we come!

I was working in Baltimore, so I had a shorter commute than Washington DC, but it was still a good hour away, so I'd ask if our construction meetings for Leg Up could happen really early in the morning. No one loved Friday morning meetings in the middle of winter at sun-up, but hey, we were building! Woo hoo! This was an awesome time—when I could finally see the dreams and vision I had put on paper for more than ten years become real.

Even the freaky weather—three feet of snow, way earlier than normal—couldn't slow us down. The building was under roof, and the crews kept working and working, speeding towards meeting the date of the opening in the spring.

With the building taking shape, it was decision time for my family and me. We had a huge choice to make. Could I leave my career and run Leg Up Farm? Or would I be ready to stand on the sidelines and watch once the Farm was up and running? How could I entrust the leadership of this center that I was so passionate about to another person? These were questions I was having a hard time answering. And okay, I just wanted the job!

I turned in my resignation from the Board so I could apply for the top position at Leg Up Farm. It was pretty scary, I'll tell you! I mean, the Board could have said no. At that moment, for the first time in twelve years, I truly had no control of the very next step! All evening I kept my eye on my cell phone, waiting for the chairman's call.

It was eight p.m.: no phone call yet. Soon it was 8:30, then 9:00: still nothing. By 9:30 I could hardly sit still. I put the phone in my pocket so I would know the second it rang. I checked my email. I waited some more. I paced. At 9:45, it finally rang. I was relieved when I saw Doug's number come up. Now, either way, I would know. Either way, the center would be built and would open. But me? I wanted to be in the midst of it.

Doug was calling to tell me the Board had made it official: I was the President & CEO of Leg Up Farm. I was pumped! As always, I celebrated for two minutes and then thought, *What's next?* Maybe I am nuts, but I dug right in—literally.

I pictured myself behind a nice desk…but my first duty was weed-whacking along the road because the township had called to say the grass was too high.

I started working. After 15 minutes, I was overjoyed to see a retired man coming across the street with his own weed-whacker. We set to work and cleared all 1,000 feet of our grass-lined roadway. The fact that he came out kept me going. By way of thanks, I handed him a Leg Up Farm baseball cap, which he promptly stuck on his head. Charlie, who still lives near the Farm, helps us out with event parking to this day.

Back at home, Laurie was supportive. She never said anything against this huge move or the pay cut it meant for our family, but I knew she was nervous about the risk of me leaving my job.

At that point we had never served a child, and we had never collected one dollar of therapy revenue. We were taking on debt building our center, and there were no guarantees. Emotions aside, I had always been focused on the next step in the vision, and this now seemed like the next logical step. But failure was not an option. We were so close, and too many children needed Leg Up Farm.

With two children in college and two children with special healthcare needs, how could I leave my management position? Our income would change drastically, and the financial security we had would be history. It was very hard for Laurie, and it was daunting even for me. But she knew that, in my heart, I had to do it.

I resigned my position as Director of Sales at Comcast Spotlight, and became the second permanent paid employee of Leg Up Farm. The building was due to open — really, this time — in the spring of 2010.

Just one more hurdle during construction!

In April 2010, we finally opened Leg Up Farm's main therapy building. *We opened!* It was such a great moment. Watching the faces of the people walking in made us all a little giddy.

It would have been nice if we could have just sat back and enjoyed it for a while. After 13 years I could have used a break. We celebrated, but we couldn't stop moving the entire vision forward. There were other awesome therapies to add, like play therapy, dance, and music—but first, we had to get those horses ready!

Fourteen days after we opened, we began construction on the next phase of the dream: the riding arena and barn.

20
A New Vision

"It was something we knew was a possibility, but we didn't want to get our hopes up. The first time we went, I took pictures with my phone and emailed them to everyone we knew, all the people who have dreamed with us, to say 'We're here! It's open. The dream came true.'"

Krista Cunningham, Parent

As I look around Leg Up Farm, my heart is full today. Kids are all over the facility—whether they are getting therapy or not. Brothers, sisters, parents…they all seem to thrive here in this kid-friendly, family-friendly environment. It makes the long, long journey worth it.

Naturally, there are still issues. Will we really be able to pull off the next phases? Will we really ever have a restaurant and assisted living facilities? I believe we will. We'll definitely try, as long as angels and supporters keep stepping up and helping us get there.

Will we be able to keep the Farm going? Will we be able to break even? Will we be able to continue to expand? Will there be other champions—ones who will adopt a horse, sponsor a kid for camp, or—my favorite fantasy—pay off that five million dollar loan that still keeps me up at night? A guy can hope, right?

There are other questions as well. Will our amazing staff stay? Or, in this field where consistency and relationships are so important, will we continually cope with turnover?

And then there's Brooke. She's come a long way. It's easier now that she goes to Leg Up Farm—and it's much simpler coordinating her therapy and school. Our family is together there a lot, and everyone finds something to do that is enjoyable. Of course, I usually end up working…but in my case it's a good thing that it's all started to blur together. I feel like my life is more whole.

Brooke is able to say a few words now, but she still struggles to do things that most of us do without thinking. She can't help splashing her face when trying to drink from a cup, for example, because her movements are so jerky. But, the great trooper that she is, she laughs at herself, because she's doing what she can and we are *so proud* of her.

Something that really makes my day is watching Brooke, who can ride horses now. I can see her joy when she's up in the saddle—she loves that she can do something just like her brother and sisters can.

Brooke at the reins.

I know Brooke loves Leg Up Farm and is proud of her daddy. I can see it in her eyes as we crest the hill and Leg Up Farm becomes visible out the car door. She perks up and has a big smile on her face.

I believe one day she will talk and share her amazing story with me. All of those things she has wanted to tell me over the years about being trapped inside her body: what she loves, what makes her sad, and what she dreams about for the future. It is going to happen. I believe in that dream!

On the last day of August 2012, under a bright blue sky, dotted with a few showy clouds, I watched as we turned on the waterfall in our new therapeutic Koi pond. Brooke rocked wildly with excitement. She was giving me her approval—in her own way—for the next great addition so many children at Leg Up Farm will enjoy.

Brooke's not always communicative in ways that other people can understand. But I often pass her in the hallway as I give tours, and she gazes up at me. She gets it. She knows that, if it weren't for her, the Farm wouldn't be here. She understands that kids are happier because she inspired this place.

Our family has been so blessed by Leg Up Farm. We would never have been able to enjoy Brooke's therapy if we had been rushing off to different appointments, spending hours in generic waiting rooms.

I have a new career that I love. At this point, I could never imagine doing anything else; nothing would be as rewarding. I love my life and work at Leg Up Farm, surrounded by the angels who have helped to build and run this amazing place.

Afterword
Always Get Back Up

*"You need to make time for your family
no matter what happens in your life."*

Matthew Quick

When you have children with special needs, every day can be a matter of life and death. Despite the success of Leg Up Farm, we continue to struggle with the day-to-day reality of two children who need more care than the others.

It was when I was in the midst of dealing with the loan for Leg Up Farm when our youngest daughter, Lauren, ended up in the emergency room.

For the past few days, she had gotten cramps and become sick to her stomach every time after she ate. Lauren lay on the couch for two days, wrapped in a blanket, not wanting to move. Laurie took her, along with Brooke, to our pediatrician, who immediately sent her to the hospital. Lauren's blood sugar was freakishly high—over 600; normal would be about 80-120.

Fortunately I was still working in Baltimore, so I was able to meet them at nearby Sinai Hospital. Lauren's grandmother, Chris, drove down to the ER and took Brooke home.

Laurie arrived at the hospital in the early afternoon, and all evening doctors and nurses hustled in and out of her cubicle, curtains scraping the room dividers with their metal rings. They settled on a diagnosis fairly quickly: Lauren had Type I diabetes.

Lauren stayed there all week as they stabilized her blood sugar and taught us how to manage the disease. Laurie and I took turns sleeping at the hospital and taking care of Brooke at home, trying to keep things as normal as possible for both daughters.

When it was my turn to be in charge of bedtime, I would put on sweatpants and my SpongeBob Square Pants shirt (Lauren had gotten me this for my birthday when she was five). I guess the nurses in the pediatric floor kind of get used to the parents doing this, but it still felt a bit odd.

I'd bring a suit and shower in the bathroom in Lauren's room. It was weird to shower and shave at the hospital…and then leave my little girl to go work, but as all parents know, when your kids are sick, you do what you have to do.

In the morning, Laurie got Brooke off to school and then drove to the hospital where we would trade places. She stayed with Lauren all day while I worked. The third shift was Laurie's mom; she'd drive down to Sinai in the afternoon so we could pick up Brooke from school, get fresh clothes, and trade schedules yet again. It didn't take long until all three of us were physically and mentally exhausted.

After Lauren came home, we settled into the new normal. Everything was fine for a few years, but one night in March, I heard yelling.

"Call 911, call 911!" I was jarred awake to the sound of these words and jumped out of bed. I stood next to my bed for a few seconds, dazed, wearing only my boxer shorts. I looked around for some clue, my head spinning.

More screaming. My heart began to race. What was going on?

A pounding noise, coming toward me. It was Laurie running down the steps. She was racing to find the emergency injection needed to raise Lauren's blood sugar if it plummeted. It had been four years since she had been diagnosed with Type I diabetes. We'd never had to use the glucagon shot, but we had several on hand—just in case. I chased Laurie back up the dark stairs to figure out what was happening and I saw Lauren's limp body, lying sideways. My wife was leaning over her, trying to figure out how to use the shot.

Our dogs, Bella and Allie, were pacing and in the way. They knew something was wrong and wanted to help. I shooed them out of the room and pressed in close to Lauren's bed. Laurie seemed unaware of me and kept screaming, "Lauren, wake up, stay with me!"

I was in shock, seeing my little girl unconscious. I touched Lauren's head and she felt cold, but she was wet with perspiration. I peeked under her eyelids and saw they were vacant. My thoughts flew in every direction. We were losing her!

I ran downstairs to call 911, and Laurie inserted the large needle into Lauren's arm. The ambulance hadn't come yet; the operator was patiently asking for our address. My fists clenched, knowing our phone number would have shown on her screen. *Stop wasting time!* I wanted to shout.

I was stuck downstairs on our land line, feeling a hundred miles away. Finally the operator said help was on its way, and I hung up and grabbed Laurie's cell from the silent kitchen.

I raced through our bedroom, grabbing a crumpled t-shirt and a pair of shorts off the floor. My cellphone lay next to my bed as it always did, since Lauren checked her blood sugar late every night and I had to be reachable. I picked it up and flew back upstairs.

The 911 operator called Laurie's cell. I handed it to Laurie, who ordered me to call the hospital. We knew the number by heart.

I was on the phone with the on-call endocrinologist, who asked whether we had any icing. Icing is ideal, because the sugar can be absorbed quickly into the body through the lining of the mouth even if the person is unconscious. I ran down to our game room and found icing among our diabetic supplies, surrounded by piles of papers tracking Lauren's food intake, insulin, and blood sugar numbers.

Upstairs, Laurie rolled Lauren's limp body onto her side again. I put icing in the side of her mouth between her cheek and gum. A trickle of blood made me jump until I realized I had sliced my finger on her braces.

It was now 12:20 a.m., 20 minutes into our emergency. The glucagon and icing had yet to have any effect. My thoughts, when they were coherent, slipped between memories of the giggling, silly girl that was Lauren and the fear that she was fading and there was nothing I could do.

I asked the doctor if we could give her another glucagon shot. She said yes. I ran back downstairs, and began to rummage through every book bag, gym bag, kitchen drawer and anywhere the glucagon could be hiding. Normally I was the finder of the family. But tonight my hands kept coming up empty.

My heart pounding, my shaking hands finally recognized the long thin shape in Lauren's volleyball bag. I dashed upstairs. Laurie gave Lauren the second shot. Nothing. We looked at each other in shock.

Laurie called her friends for prayer, while I sat with Lauren. Her eyes were glazed over and she was unresponsive. *Where were the paramedics?*

After 25 minutes, Lauren's blood glucose number rose slightly. She briefly opened her eyes, but didn't know what was happening.

I felt hope for the first time since I'd heard Laurie screaming. I had rarely seen Laurie cry, but tonight she had screamed and cried out loud, as if she could call Lauren back from wherever our little girl was hiding.

Help finally arrived at 12:35 a.m. Moments after the paramedics had arrived, Lauren had opened her eyes once more. The three paramedics stood in Lauren's bedroom as I tested her blood sugar. Magic was what I had been hoping for, but the paramedics' bags of medical gear lay at their feet unopened.

Why aren't they doing anything?

The five of us stood, tense and silent, poised for action as I checked the reading. Again, it had risen, but just slightly. I looked over at the paramedics, who exchanged a glance. When they nodded and relaxed, I knew Lauren would be okay.

Her skin was still cold, but she was drenched in sweat. She opened her eyes again and, shakily, sat up as I supported her body. I held a straw up to her lips and she sipped a little orange juice, then sagged against me. *Hooray*, I said in my exhausted mind … we are all going to be all right.

Laurie closed her eyes, clasped her hands, glanced upward in a moment of thanks, and sank slowly to Lauren's side. Tears streamed down her cheeks, and my eyes filled as well. I gave her a tiny smile.

We bundled Lauren in blankets. At last able to speak, she kept repeating, "I'm freezing!" She lay back down, exhausted, barely able to move.

The paramedics told us stories to pass the time as we waited for Lauren to recover and for the doctor, who was still on the phone, to give the okay for them to leave.

They asked Lauren the standard questions: How old are you? When is your birthday? She was foggy, but replied, "14," and, haltingly, "March 2". Laurie and I were ecstatic at these simple signs of life.

Eventually Lauren's blood sugar rose to 80, and the paramedics were cleared to go. Laurie took the phone into the hallway, discussing the situation with the doctor.

I knew what she was asking: *Could what had happened tonight cause any long-term damage to Lauren's organs or brain?* We couldn't understand why this had happened to our girl. *She's an athlete,* we reasoned, *she eats well. What did she do to deserve this?*

The rest of the night we were reluctant to leave Lauren's side. Drained physically and mentally after the ups and downs of adrenalin, we settled ourselves on the other twin bed in her room. But sleep? We didn't dare.

Every 15 minutes, then every 30 minutes, then every hour, we checked Lauren's blood sugar. By 4:00 a.m. Lauren's fingers must have had 50 pinpricks in them. Her fingertips are scarred from years of doing this, but we had never seen them as bad as they were that night.

Laurie and I replayed every second of what had happened. We had been fortunate that Laurie had stayed on the couch to make sure Lauren was okay before settling in for the night. *What if she hadn't?*

A few days later Laurie and Lauren went to a volleyball tournament in Baltimore and learned that another player had died 11 days before the tournament from the same situation; she had been Lauren's age.

Apparently the girl had been tucked into bed at 11:00 p.m. When her parents had gone to wake her up the next morning at 6:30, they realized that she had died during the night. Their schedule mirrored the ritual we had followed every day — before that night.

What if this happens again while we are asleep? We couldn't bear the thought of leaving Lauren's side, but would it be fair to our other children? Would it even be do-able to stand by her side every moment of the day?

We were used to these kinds of fears because of Brooke. Now we would fear for both daughters. It is so hard for me to know that I have no way to make things better for either of my girls.

Every night since then, Laurie and I wake up to test Lauren's blood sugar at midnight, 2:00 a.m., 4:00 a.m., and then again when she gets up for school at 6:00 a.m. This is the minimum number of tests—as long as her blood sugar numbers are normal. Otherwise one of us sleeps in the twin bed in Lauren's room, waking up every 15 minutes if necessary for her safety…and to assuage our fears.

Laurie is tired…every day. I'm concerned about the long-term effects of her not sleeping. I'm concerned for everyone in our home. I try to be strong for my family, because I think if they see me panic, it will make things worse. So on the inside, I ache, but on the outside, I try to model hope and fearlessness.

As our family spends more time together at Leg Up Farm, we have learned that we're not alone with these types of emergencies. Many of the families who come there have spent scary moments waiting for an ambulance or listening very closely to the sounds of their children breathing at night.

We bond over things like these, and just feeling the strength of the new community that surrounds us now gives us a sense of courage that buoys us when those terrifying moments come flooding into our lives. We even talk about it with each other, telling each other the silly things that happen in the middle of those late-night adventures, and knowing it's good for us to be able to laugh about them.

As we watch our children flourish at Leg Up Farm, we find times of refreshment. We are together in a safe place, a healing place, enjoying the simple things that happen every day. Thanks to a thousand small signs of hope, we regain the ability once again to have the courage to dream and we cherish every moment of time with all of the special people in our lives.

Lauren & Daddy.

Acknowledgments

First, I thank the Lord for helping me understand the purpose for my life. To my family, thank you for helping to shape my life and give it meaning! I am grateful to you for teaching me about God and teaching me to love and genuinely care about others.

To my board and staff, I couldn't have done this without you. And the pages written in this book would not have been possible without the observant eyes of: my daughters Olivia & Lauren Castriota, and Cindy Kalinoski & her daughter Elena.

The pages of this book are not big enough to capture all of the amazing people who have helped me on this journey to build Leg Up Farm. This is the best way I can find to recognize everyone: if I have ever met you and we talked about Leg Up Farm, you can be certain that *you* helped make this special place possible. You shaped my thoughts and opinions. Whether you encouraged me or discouraged me, you helped me grow. My actions were led by you, and all of these connections are woven through every essence of Leg Up Farm and our success today.

In this book you have read about just a few of the very special people who lent a hand—I call them angels. They came along at a time when I needed help. As you pursue your own dream, look around you. Where are your angels? I'll bet they're there, waiting for you to voice your dream. And as you do, you'll discover that nothing is impossible for those who believe in their own unique dream.

Laurie, Lauren, Brooke, Louie, Olivia & Toby, 2011.

About Leg Up Farm

This family-focused center provides children with special needs and their families a comprehensive range of therapies under one roof, regardless of their ability to pay. Serving over a thousand families, Leg Up Farm is a LEED-certified facility offering science-based therapeutic care, incorporating equine, educational, horticultural, physical, speech, occupational and other therapies. It also features the country's largest barrier-free Koi pond.

To learn more about Leg Up Farm, or to donate, go to: *www.LegUpFarm.org*. There, you can:

- Symbolically adopt a horse, or Isaiah the donkey
- Sponsor a child for therapy or camp
- Help fund the planned therapy pool
- Get your name on a sign in our riding arena
- Develop a business activity for Matthew's Town
- Ask for information on starting your own Leg Up Farm

September 9th, 2009

Lauren Castriota

Welcome to our groundbreaking of leg up Farm. My name is Lauren Castriota and my dad, Lou Castriota, is the creator and founder of this soon to be unique physycility. In my life 2 people are my inspesations and this physility's too. One of the two is my dad. He is amazing not only as a father, but as a worker. He dedicates most of his time here at leg up farm wether it's doing work like weed waking or it's just taking a stroll on the site to see how it's coming along with the help of you and our amazing team of volenteers working on their time, for children needing a leg up in life. The other person that is truly my best friend and an inspesation to all I do, is my sister Brooke. Brooke got a midochondrial desiese as a baby and eversince has been a inspesation to me by always passervering and keeping a smile on her face no matter what her struggles are. In our lives we all have struggles but no matter how hard it gets for you, plenty more people have it worse. So the next time you have a bad day just remember focus your energy on helping someone else, that always makes me feel better.

Thank you for your time and effort to put this project in to action.